"This book looks to a bright future for the Amer[...] with Jesus as the beating heart at the [...] and ministry provide a model of [...] foretaste of the great possibilities [...] part in Jesus's life, with him as ou[...] friend. Steve has put his heart into [...], and I hope Christians will read it, consider it, and take up his call to 'obedience to the way of Jesus.'"

—**Michael Wear**, founder, president, and CEO, Center for Christianity and Public Life; author of *The Spirit of Our Politics: Spiritual Formation and the Renovation of Public Life*

"This is an altar call for the American church. With his wise, skillful, and learned pastoral voice, Steve Bezner calls us to come to Jesus just as we are—leaving behind the trappings of our power and privilege. He reminds us, drawing from his experience as a Texas pastor, that the kingdom Jesus calls us to is diverse, loving, and more focused on people than on material wealth and power. This is a book I will give to my friends, family, and fellow ministry leaders. It is a book to which I fervently pray we will listen."

—**Beth Allison Barr**, professor, Baylor University; bestselling author of *The Making of Biblical Womanhood*

"Not many would want to be a prophetic voice today. There can be a cost to speaking out, but doing so means that you are unbought. That is what you will sense in these pages by my brother Steve Bezner. You may get rattled or even triggered at times, but that is not a bad thing. The American church has become too politics-centered rather than Christ-centered. We need a biblical worldview more than ever today. Read this work and experience the growth and implementation of such a vision."

—**Eric Mason**, senior pastor, Epiphany Fellowship

"*Your Jesus Is Too American* tackles the most pressing issues causing tension among Americans today. The reasons behind why Steve is a good pastor are the same reasons why this book is timely: they are informed, intuitive, intelligent, intimate, and invested. During this divided and fragmented time, Steve calls us to hold fast to the Jesus of the Bible."

—**Daniel Yang**, national director of Churches of Welcome

"Rarely does a book jump off the page like this one. Steve's ability to write in a way that can be absorbed and practiced by anyone is truly a gift. The kingdom of God is still coming; there is nothing more hopeful, revolutionary, or transformational to our current personal and societal context than this. It's odd how we've become masters of helping people accept Jesus without teaching much else. Steve takes us beyond accepting Christ to embracing what he taught."

—**Bob Roberts Jr.**, senior pastor, author, and president of Multi-Faith Neighbors Network and Institute for Global Engagement

"Offering pastoral words from a pastoral presence, *Your Jesus Is Too American* is a book we need today. With echoes of Bonhoeffer's prophetic call to Christians from nearly a century ago, Steve Bezner draws us with tenderness and strength to the One in whom we find our identity. A beautiful book."

—**Lore Ferguson Wilbert**, author of *The Understory, A Curious Faith*, and *Handle with Care*

"Whatever you may think is at the root of our current cultural crisis, the only solution for the Christian must be a radical recommitment to the way of Jesus Christ. The beautiful—and challenging—brilliance of Steve Bezner's *Your Jesus Is Too American* is that it presses us to face the fullness of Christ's teaching, and it presses us to believe it."

—**Jared C. Wilson**, assistant professor and author in residence, Midwestern Seminary; pastor for preaching, Liberty Baptist Church, Liberty, Missouri; author of *Friendship with the Friend of Sinners*

YOUR JESUS IS TOO AMERICAN

Calling the Church to Reclaim Kingdom Values over the American Dream

Steve Bezner

FOREWORD BY BETH MOORE

BrazosPress

a division of Baker Publishing Group
Grand Rapids, Michigan

To Joy,
the one who has loved me
most like Jesus

Published by Brazos Press
a division of Baker Publishing Group
Grand Rapids, Michigan
BrazosPress.com

Printed in the United States of America

Library of Congress Cataloging-in-Publication Data
Names: Bezner, Steven M., author.
Title: Your Jesus is too American : calling the church to reclaim kingdom values over the American dream / Steve Bezner.
Description: Grand Rapids, Michigan : Brazos Press, a division of Baker Publishing Group, [2024] | Includes bibliographical references.
Identifiers: LCCN 2024008558 | ISBN 9781587436314 (paperback) | ISBN 9781587436512 (casebound) | ISBN 9781493447862 (ebook)
Subjects: LCSH: Church renewal—United States. | Christianity and culture—United States. | Church and social problems—United States. | Church and the world. | United States—Moral conditions. | Evangelicalism—United States.
Classification: LCC BV600.3 .B485 2024 | DDC 262.001/70973—dc23/eng/20240317
LC record available at https://lccn.loc.gov/2024008558

Cover design by Laura Powell
Author photo by Melanie Beddow

The author is represented by The Christopher Ferebee Agency, www.christopherferebee.com.

Baker Publishing Group publications use paper produced from sustainable forestry practices and postconsumer waste whenever possible.

24 25 26 27 28 29 30   7 6 5 4 3 2 1

★ CONTENTS ★

★ FOREWORD ★

Beth Moore

The first time I heard Steve Bezner preach, I reached into my purse to pull out a pen, squinted stage-ward to study him carefully, and thought, *Where's this guy been?* I'd been part of our city's diverse Christian community for forty years. I knew—and loved—a lot of gifted preachers, especially of Steve's denomination. I didn't know how I'd missed this one. This guy at the pulpit was a marvelous mix of brilliance, warmth, truth-telling, humility, and generosity of grace. He appeared to be both studied and Spirit-imbued. A wise preacher knows all the preparation in the world can't make up for the absence of God's anointing. Nor will God let a communicator get along indefinitely exploiting anointing to avoid preparation.

Ironically, Steve and I were already friends by the time I heard him preach. Fellow Houstonians, we came to know one another serving a community neck-deep in the muddy waters of Hurricane Harvey. He'd also gotten my attention on social media as a pastor who spoke what he believed to be right, just, and true, even when he knew he'd lose the favor of people in high ecclesiastical places. As I look back on it now, I can so clearly see that what made his voice different from the louder public discourse was his cage-rattling gospel consistency. From my point of view, Steve seemed to be suspiciously lacking in blind spots, like someone who'd once been cloudy-eyed but had since spent a good bit of time with an expert ophthalmologist.

Dr. Bezner certainly was no secret to his community. The parking lot of the church he oversaw was packed every open Sunday. The only way I know to explain how the secret was kept from me is that God, in his mercy, saved Steve's preaching for a season I'd need it most.

This is as good a time as any to share one of my biggest frustrations with God. He is annoyingly uncooperative with my categorizing. Right about then, and for the first time in my life, I was suffering from an excruciatingly low estimation of evangelical preachers. The thing about typecasting is that it's not only sinful, it's also lazy. It's easier to dismiss a whole group and say they're all a bunch of whatevers than develop actual discernment. The depth of my low estimation of a certain company of preachers was matched only by the inordinate height of my estimation before my crisis.

That I've found any semblance of balance in this season of reevaluating everything but Jesus is, in part, due to God putting Steve Bezner and men like him on my radar. What I have so deeply appreciated in his teaching is beautifully captured here in his writing. You will be taught, not talked down to. You will be served, not seduced by someone seeking celebrity. And if by chance you find yourself offended by something he says, hear him out. Hear the gospel he preaches, and thank

God for people who are brave enough to speak truths that hurt, because only truth can heal. Thank God for those who make us question whether our outlook is Christlike or culturally Christian.

In closing, I'd like to say that writing a book is risky business. You scratch and claw against your own maddening proclivity to distraction, clamoring to find that magic moment when time and a few clear thoughts align. You construct phrases and sentences from a present state of mind, health, and circumstances that feel deceptively permanent, then hand them into an editorial team that hacks the flourish from them and improves the writing against what you're often convinced is your better judgment. *It was good like it was.* No, it wasn't, but thankfully, you're not the publisher's first rodeo and, if they're worth their salaries, they're heck-bent on saving you from yourself.

Finally, a generally agreed-upon manuscript emerges, but you've only now arrived at the trickiest part: it rolls to press into a future you're hoping is vaguely relevant to what you've written. We're trying to stay afoot on a frantically spinning top, in a fractured world perpetually changing, charged by electrifying fear. We go to sleep with the absolute certainty of uncertainty. If we who are of faith didn't believe we were doing God's will to the best of our understanding, publishing a book would be like betting a year's pay on a horse named Hit-or-Miss.

What we of faith in Christ *do* have is an unchanging God, an indestructible gospel, the indwelling Holy Spirit, and the God-breathed Scriptures. To these we take our tumultuous times. To these we take our confusion. To these we take our divisions. To these we run when we don't know where to turn or who to trust.

To these this book will take you.

For believers in Jesus, going forward is always about going back. It's about having the humility to ask ourselves and our communities of faith, "At what point did we lose our way to have ended up here?" It's about jumping off the crazy train of which side's right and which side's wrong. Mortals are too fraught to hold opinions without error, too wrong about our neighbors to trust our gut with their highest good. This side of the veil, perceptions appear as realities. Feelings swear they're telling the truth.

But, in our most rational moments, don't we know somewhere down deep that where we sit determines what we see? That's why this book is worth our while. It camps us at the feet of Jesus, where he's all we can see until our vision improves enough to view others as God's image bearers rather than "trees walking" (Mark 8:24).

What we're looking for is a way of living, loving, neighboring, worshiping, working, serving, and ultimately dying that is, in Paul's words, "in step with the truth of the gospel" (Gal. 2:14). That is the way of freedom. We have pledged our allegiance to our personal rights and found ourselves more lacking than ever, misled by celebrity, bled dry by self-interest. We need more than our human best. We need Jesus. Beautifully, to the degree we'll own our need of him, we will have him.

Christ loves the church. He's doing us good. He has illuminated our disillusionment in recent years so that, in his light, we see light (Ps. 36:9). He is allowing our idols to come crashing down—one after another—and our corrupt systems to fail us so that we'll finally get too weary to rebuild them. By all means, let us throw up our hands in frustrated, freeing surrender. For only Jesus saves.

★ ACKNOWLEDGMENTS ★

I have never written a book before, and I have no idea if I will ever have the opportunity to write another one, so I find myself very worried about writing this section for fear that I will forget to thank or mention someone. I have no doubt that I will, in fact, forget someone, so I hope that you'll forgive the oversights and simply know how grateful I am to have had the opportunity to see this book in print and how thankful I am for all of those who have encouraged me along the way.

I'll begin where Katelyn Beaty told me to begin—by thanking God. I often thought about writing a book, but I never felt like I knew what to write about. One day I felt a nudge from the Spirit telling me to write a book about the kingdom. The nudge was so strong that I knew if I did not do so, I would be disobeying the Lord, so I set about the process. I know that sounds like something a pastor would say, but it is true.

Many people have taught me about what it means to faithfully follow Jesus over the years. First and foremost, my parents, in-laws, and grandparents have modeled this for me. They showed me how to live faithfully, and a few have shown me how to die in the same manner. I am grateful for each of them.

Along the way, the Lord provided people who modeled faithful living, and I want to mention a few of them specifically. Brent Gentzel, Beth Moore, and Bob Roberts have each been gifts from God in helping me follow the way of Jesus. I also want to thank those who taught me how to think theologically: James Shields (now with the Lord), Ron Smith (who introduced me to theology), and Barry Harvey (who taught me to rightly read Bonhoeffer).

The people of Houston Northwest Church have been incredibly gracious to me in this process. They listened as I worked through my thoughts on the kingdom, and they helped me refine that thinking by asking excellent questions. I am much more a pastor than I am a writer, so I could not have begun to communicate these things without such a marvelous congregation. The elders of our church have been patient with me as well, allowing me to tackle issues that aren't always popular to hear from the pulpit—to varying degrees of success. Wade Brehm, Darren Carver, Dwight Davis, Kirk Gentzel, Nate Gordon, David Hodgins, Bruce Hurst, Terry Lechinger, Cory Quarles, John Roberts, Bill Roberts, Steve Rutledge, Stuart Sheehan, Allen Tate, Dobie Weise, and Dan Worrell have been incredibly supportive during this writing process and throughout my pastorate.

Likewise, our church staff have had to deal with me being unavailable for questions while I tried to meet writing deadlines. To Emily Bass, Galen Blom, Michelle Bundy, Abby Cazares, Adrian Cazares, Clint Collins, Matt Delp, Sarah Delp, Kristin DePue, Leslie Espinosa, Megan Fisackerly, Priscilla Fletcher, Chris Flores, Chris Hall, Julie Hernandez, Don Howard, Aaron Lloyd, Karla Longoria, Joel Loveless, Marilyn

Maddox, Jared McGuire, Melissa Money, Tiffany Moore, Rohan Mundle, Shawn Myers, Cassidy Odom, Tara Powell, Kelsey Price, Lisa Prins, Rose Rodriguez, and Bethany Scott: I am grateful to call you my friends—as well as my coworkers.

A few friends told me I was not crazy and that, yes, I should actually write a book. Thanks to Joshua Jones, Jeff Medders, Brandon Smith, David and Michelle Smith, Molly Stillman, Lore Wilbert, and Jared Wilson for the kind push.

I am also thankful for the many friends and family members who did not roll their collective eyes when I talked about the book in the course of casual conversation. The entire Bezner/Mays/Young clan, Aaron and Hannah Bunker, Andy and Natalie Evans, Jason Farquhar, Jonathan and Lindsay Gay, Kerra Gentzel, Joel and Sarah Goza, Emily Greer, Eric and Allison Leatherwood, Mike and Ashley Milford, Gene and Nancy Morisak, Britt and Jennifer Murrey, Dustin Odom, John and Lori Redfearn, Nate Wilbert, and Gretchen Worrell—you each have encouraged me in different ways over the years. I am so thankful for you.

My siblings have had the unique experience of having a pastor for a brother. To Chris, Duston, Jenna, Jeremy, and Michelle: thanks for putting up with that oddity all these years. I love each of you.

The Lord has created a rich community of pastors in Houston, and I want to thank each of them for spurring me to live a life faithful to Jesus, particularly when I have teetered on the edge. There are far too many to list, but I must thank Duane Brooks, David Fleming, Curtis Jones, Bryant Lee, Aaron Lutz, Justin Moore, Jeremiah Morris, Roger Patterson, Matt Roberson, Ryan Rush, Billy Schiel, Lawrence Scott, Jason Shepperd, Jarrett Stephens, Jeff Wells, Ken Werlein, Bruce Wesley, and Blake Wilson. Additionally, I'm thankful for my Glocalnet pastor friends who have walked with me in my toughest moments: Kevin Brown, Nic Burleson, Kevin Cox, Micah Fries, Brian Haynes, Mitch Jolly, Daniel Langford, Joel Rainey, Kevin Seaman, Scott Venable, and Daniel Yang, I thank God for each of you.

Having never written a book before, I was likely a bit of an extra burden for the people on the business side of this process. Thank you, Beth Allison Barr for asking Katelyn Beaty to consider my work. Thanks to Katelyn Beaty at Brazos Press for giving me frank feedback and excellent advice—and for making me laugh. She's funny, y'all. Many thanks as well to the entire Brazos team for making the process as smooth as possible for a rookie, particularly Erin Smith, Julie Zahm, and Ryan Davis. I'm also very thankful for Angela Scheff for becoming my agent and answering my (often clueless) questions. She helped me every step of the way. I had no idea what I was doing, but she treated me like a professional nevertheless.

Finally, I want to thank my family. My sons, Ben and Drew, have often had to endure their father not being available. Such is the life of the pastor's family. Despite this, they each have grown into fine men of God, and I am grateful to be called their dad. They have taught me so much about following Jesus simply by showing me how relentless God's love must be for each of us.

Last, but certainly not least, I want to thank my wife, Joy. She knows every single one of my failings, and yet she is— and always has been—my greatest cheerleader. Joy, I love you more than I could ever adequately express. Thanks for loving me the way Jesus does. I hope my life reflects the love toward you that I feel in my heart.

Hidden Treasure

(Re)Discovering Jesus Values

The kingdom of heaven is like treasure, buried in a field, that a man found and reburied. Then in his joy he goes and sells everything he has and buys that field.

—Matthew 13:44

And here I have found what I sought not indeed, but finding I would possess forever. For it is above all gold and silver, and beyond all jewels.

—J. R. R. Tolkien, *The Silmarillion*

This is a book about obedience to the way of Jesus.[1] It is also a book about how the way of Jesus often stands in stark contrast with the American way.

1. The origins of this book stem from a sermon series preached at Houston Northwest Church in 2022 titled "The Backwards Way of Jesus." The current title, *Your Jesus Is Too American*, is a nod to Jared C. Wilson's 2009 book, *Your Jesus Is Too Safe*. That book happened to be Jared's first book as well. Jared is an excellent theologian and a far better writer than I am, but I hope, in a

In the 1930s, the German pastor Dietrich Bonhoeffer wrote a book about obedience to the way of Jesus called *Nachfolge*, which means "following."[2] In Bonhoeffer's day, wild allegiance to the National Socialists—popularly known as the Nazis—flourished. Nationalism was on the rise. Immigrants, Jews, and citizens with special needs and physical handicaps were targeted in both speeches and official policy. Amid this increasing nationalism, Germans focused on strength: they wanted to leave behind the shame of losing World War I and become an unconquerable force.

The German church was caught up in the hysteria. The church was an official extension of the government, and soon the German bishop was participating in Nazi propaganda, saluting the Führer, and taking advantage of photo opportunities with him. Church posters featured crosses bent into swastikas. Church altars were draped with Nazi flags. National symbolism and religious symbolism were combined into an indistinguishable entity.[3]

Surrounded by this confusion, Bonhoeffer was one of the pastors who recognized that many German Christians were finding meaning and purpose (and perhaps their idea of salvation) from national identity rather than from following Jesus. Hitler was seen as a savior—as God's vessel chosen to bring honor back to Germany. The category of national

manner of speaking, to build on the vision he articulated in these pages. His writing ministered to me when I was in a very dark place, and I will always be grateful.

2. Most Americans know this book by the title *The Cost of Discipleship*.

3. I first became aware of the entangling of the German church and government during this period as a young man who was interested in Dietrich Bonhoeffer and looking through a pictorial history of his life. It was there that I saw the propaganda posters of crosses turned into swastikas and flag-draped altars. See Renate Bethge and Christian Gremmels, eds., *Dietrich Bonhoeffer: A Life in Pictures*, centenary ed. (Minneapolis: Fortress, 2006).

identity was, for many, a far more satisfying mantle than that of the itinerant rabbi from Nazareth.

Bonhoeffer wrote *Nachfolge* as a warning to the church of his day. He returned to the words of Jesus, specifically the Gospel of Matthew, and tried to show how following Jesus was completely different from following the power-hungry ways of his nation.

I would never compare myself to Bonhoeffer, and this book is likely not destined to become a spiritual classic like *Nachfolge*. I do, however, notice at least one similarity between many American Christians and the German Christians in Bonhoeffer's day. The American church, as a whole, struggles in finding its identity completely in Jesus. Similar to the Germans of the 1930s, American Christians often gravitate toward power or seek to align with a political party. We base our behavior more on popular culture than the prophetic words Jesus spoke. As a result, we are angrier and more divided within both our nation and our church than we have been in a very long time. As a pastor, I see firsthand how cable news and social media—not the New Testament—regularly define how American Christians think and speak. Rather than the church seasoning the culture like salt, its distinct flavor has instead been diluted by the culture.

As a result, I've written a book intended to point us back to the way of Jesus so that we recognize that following our Lord may regularly put us at odds with the power structures and common practices of our Western culture. I've aimed to do so in the way Bonhoeffer did—by returning to the words of Jesus.

I hope to show just how beautiful Jesus and his teachings are. Choosing obedience to an arcane way[4] may result in a

---

4. This is a nod to Bonhoeffer's prison writings. Bonhoeffer believed that the church should respond to the secret discipline of mystery in worship—the

revived church, renewed joy, and—let us hope—a changed world. If we rediscover who Jesus is, if we remember how great his love is for each of us, I believe we will be awakened to the deeply joyful life awaiting us.

This is a book about obedience to Jesus, but it is an obedience deeply rooted in love of Jesus. My hope is that you will feel my love of Jesus in these words and that you will sense the deep love he has for you—and for all people.

I also hope along the way we might rediscover what Jesus treasures, what he values.

In doing so, we might find that we treasure those things as well.

The church I attended growing up had a library. It wasn't all that large, and it smelled a bit musty, but it holds a magical place in my memory. I can still remember sitting on the metal footstool amid the stacks, flipping through children's books, looking for treasures. It was there that I first encountered Narnia and, by extension, C. S. Lewis. Other magical worlds opened as well. It was also there that I found a book explaining the end of the world, complete with a foldout chart.

One day while my mom looked at the books for grown-ups in the church library, I discovered another book containing a magical world—*Alice's Adventures in Wonderland*. This particular volume was a "double feature," so once I completed *Wonderland*, I dove straight into its sequel: *Through the Looking-Glass, and What Alice Found There*. For those who

---

disciplina arcani. See Dietrich Bonhoeffer, *Letters and Papers from Prison*, vol. 8 of Dietrich Bonhoeffer Works, ed. Christian Gremmels, Eberhard Bethge, and Renate Bethge, trans. Isabel Best, Lisa Dahill, Reinhard Krauss, and Nancy Lukens (Minneapolis: Fortress, 1998), 29, 32, 364, 365, 373, and 390.

have not read the book or seen a film adaptation (either the classic Disney animated feature or the visually stunning Tim Burton film), the premise of the book is simple: Alice enters a magical world by stepping through a mirror, and in this world everything is backward. (For the comic book fans among us, think of Bizarro World from *Superman*.)

While the book turns out to be a dream (or so we think), the message is clear: Alice must adapt to live within a world that is completely upside down from the world she knows. And it turns out that living in a backward world requires a good deal of work.

I am not the first person to note that the kingdom into which Jesus calls Christians to live is upside down or backward. Any number of books have been written on this topic.[5] Jesus himself pointed that out to his followers from the very beginning when he said multiple times in his Sermon on the Mount, "You have heard it said . . . but I say to you." This backward way of life was the earliest form of church growth and evangelism. By choosing, for example, to elevate women to places of significance and to care for abandoned children and sickly elders, the earliest Christians expressed their theological beliefs in a countercultural way. Through the church's backward way of living in obedience to Jesus, institutions like hospitals and orphanages were born, and, despite all odds, the church grew rapidly.

Put simply: the church's power was found in its willingness to live differently—in public.

5. The modern classic on following Jesus I find to be most influential these days is Dallas Willard, *The Divine Conspiracy: Rediscovering Our Hidden Life in God* (New York: Harper, 1998).

In recent years, however, the church has not been growing rapidly—at least not in the West. It seems each year a new demographic study emerges demonstrating that the number of American churchgoers continues to decline and that the number of people who are not committed to any religious tradition (the "nones") are on the rise, especially among younger generations.

As the Western church continues to decline in size and seeming influence, pastors and church leaders are asking one question over and over: Why?

It's a worthy question, and it will take many conversations from many perspectives to address the question adequately. Following Canadian philosopher Charles Taylor, some have suggested that the church is declining simply because of the "disenchantment" of the world and the rise of secularism.[6] Others have been wringing their hands over the rise of postmodernity and moral relativism.

To be sure, the world has shifted a great deal. Secularism, postmodernity, and moral relativism are all very real issues that the church must consider in its missional approach and identity today. I wonder, however, if most of the church's decline today is less a cultural shift and more a result of a church shift. To put it more plainly, I wonder if the church is declining in the West because the church in the West became too successful—not at discipleship or evangelism but at identifying with Western culture in a way that made the church lose its distinct personality. In our desire to remain

6. Charles Taylor's *A Secular Age* (Cambridge, MA: Belknap, 2007) is one of the most influential books to have emerged in the humanities over the last generation. Taylor's work is towering and labyrinthine in scope, yet it is worth engagement if we are to understand the spiritual and philosophical moment of the contemporary West.

relevant, we lost our difference, and, by extension, we allowed the very thing we hoped to gain to slip away.

Why did the church begin to decline at the precise moment Christians had the most cultural influence they had ever had?

My theory is that the church was successful in its earliest days—despite being a religious minority—precisely because of its cultural difference. If we look at the ancient world, it is easy to understand how Christian theology and practice differed. In the earliest days of the church, when Christians chose not to participate in Caesar worship, or refused to join a guild because of the pagan connections (thereby creating enormous professional challenges), or abstained from the prevalent sexual practices of the day, they were easy to spot.[7] Likewise, when Christians preached a message that was not based on deity appeasement but rather emphasized that the Deity had done the appeasing himself, their theology was singular.

The church grew in the first century because Christians cheerfully and faithfully embodied a set of countercultural theological beliefs. It grew because at its core was a different way of seeing the world. That difference caught the eye of many people, and it drew them into the church.

The church grew in its earliest days because it was different from the culture.

I wonder if the same could be true today. I wonder if we could live again as an influential minority.

What if our greatest power might be in our difference?

---

7. See Larry Hurtado, *Destroyer of the Gods: Early Christian Distinctiveness in the Roman World* (1996; repr., Waco: Baylor University Press, 2017) for discussions of these and other examples of Christian distinctiveness in the ancient world.

Difference alone, however, won't be enough.

Christians (and followers of other religions) are tempted to ground their difference in a mindset of battle, to think of living differently as a way to do war against the world. I can sympathize with this posture. The believers who take this sort of stance make some excellent points: the church is indeed in decline; much of the morality of the United States is almost unrecognizable from just a few generations ago. I can certainly understand why some brothers and sisters in the faith might think that the best tactic is to "go to war" for our nation, and why they adopt an almost militant mindset in their theologies and churches.

The problem with such approaches is that they tend to focus on reclaiming cultural power and influence through institutions and lawmaking instead of employing the spiritual tactics the earliest churches used—prayer and service. Yes, institutions and lawmaking are important, but the ancient church did not focus on difference so that they might overtake institutions. While I'm certain the ancient church would have enjoyed and appreciated such a reality, first-century Christians likely never envisioned a world in which the emperor would make Christianity not only legal but the official religion of the empire. They assumed the opposite and acted accordingly. Surprisingly, however, their loving acts of service and prayer had an exponential effect.

The earliest churches practiced a difference that was rooted in subtle subversion of the power structures of the day. The early confession of Christian faith, "Jesus is Lord," was a direct derivative of the pagan confession, "Caesar is Lord." This practice of subversive spiritual difference has deep roots in Scripture. From the midwives telling Pharaoh that Hebrew women were more vigorous than Egyptian women to Daniel and his friends choosing different food from the Babylonians to Jeremiah telling the exiles to seek the welfare of the city of Babylon itself, the people of God have often understood that they are at their best when they seek ordinary faithfulness by subverting expectations and choosing service rather than anger. By humbling themselves, they allow the Lord to exalt them on his timetable and in his way.

I fear that those embracing culture war will slide into the mentality of self-exaltation inevitable after conquest. If the victor both receives the spoils and is the one to write history, how can pride not follow? Scripture is clear: if we humble ourselves, the Lord will exalt us; conversely, if we exalt ourselves, the Lord will humble us. The Lord opposes the proud, and it is difficult to wage war in the physical realm without becoming prideful.

I want to suggest an alternative approach. The best sort of difference is one that can organically draw others into the faith and, by extension, increase the influence of the church. *Rather than waging war, I propose cultivating a garden.* Let us plant wheat among the tares and allow the King to separate them out. This may sound naive to some, but I believe the ancient Christians give us good reason to trust this method.

Rodney Stark's excellent book *The Rise of Christianity* shows that the early Jesus movement grew not through the pursuit of cultural power but because believers loved those who were rejected by culture. It was through demonstrations of love for women, the sick, the elderly, the abandoned, and the foreigner that people understood the wide love of God and were drawn to the message of Jesus as Messiah. The most common metaphor for church in the New Testament is family; outsiders were welcomed into churches as brothers and sisters. The early Christians planted subversive seeds of gospel embodiment through their unique ways of living. As a result, they grew to a point where the ruling authorities had no choice but to take them seriously.[8]

This inflection point proved consequential for the church, both then and now. The church moved from being marginal and subversive to being central and powerful. Stark points out how orphanages and hospitals were established and how a general concern for human rights began to take shape—albeit in nascent form—in the wake of the earliest Christian movement. As Christians loved their neighbors generously, even the powerful pagan Roman Empire saw their benefit, and the church grew in its influence, leading to the eventual joining of church and empire under the rulership of Emperor Constantine. As I will later discuss, such a close relationship led (and still leads) to a number of problems—climaxing in the church's complicated legacy in military ventures like the Crusades and taxation schemes like the selling of indulgences.

Lately, however, the church has moved closer to the margins of society. As pluralism rises in the West the church finds itself pushed into a more marginal position with declining authority. Christians in the twenty-first century, particularly those in the West, are left wondering whether the church should fight to restore its cultural power.

Perhaps an even more pressing question is this: Can the church be true to its calling when retaining power is on its mind at all?

8. Rodney Stark, *The Rise of Christianity: How the Obscure, Marginal Jesus Movement Became the Dominant Religious Force in the Western World in a Few Centuries* (San Francisco: HarperSanFrancisco, 1997).

I love America.

Yes, this country is flawed. And, yes, there have been some terrible moments in its history. I don't turn a blind eye to our legacy of slavery, racism, and violence that has been perpetrated in its name. But I also believe that America holds a sense of hopefulness for which many people yearn. I live in Houston, Texas, a global city. The last time I counted, we had almost forty nations represented in our congregation. Over one hundred languages are spoken in the homes of students in our school district. People from all over the world are excited to come to the United States because—for all its flaws—America symbolizes something special.

I proudly fly a flag in front of our house on national holidays. I've been known to tear up at particularly emotive fireworks displays on Independence Day. I find joy in thanking veterans for their service. Just last week I rearranged my schedule to watch the United States play Wales in the World Cup. Hot dogs, apple pie, pickup trucks, baseball: I love them all.

But—and this is critical—America is not the church.

An influential strain of theology within the American church has attempted to make the United States a "new Israel" of sorts and, by extension, to turn the United States into a sort of governmental religion.[9] To be clear, I have in mind here those who want to impose a more extreme vision

---

9. This theological movement sometimes goes by the title of Christian nationalism. I'll talk more about this movement and its relationship to Christian reconstructionism in chap. 7. As many have pointed out, there are competing moral visions in our nation, and each ought to have the opportunity to lobby for their preferences in the public square. I am more concerned with the movement which tends toward theocratic extremism.

of theocracy, *not* Christians who want to participate in the democratic process (such participation is vital). Those who employ this theocratic line of thinking have historical reasons for their position, many of them overlapping with the concerns of mainstream Christian political engagement, which is why parsing out this particular line of political argumentation is not always simple. For example, many of the early colonists to our shores used this sort of language in searching for a place where they might find the freedom to worship without oppression. And, to be sure, many of those who served in founding roles for our nation viewed the creation of the United States through a theological lens. Furthermore, at least one modern philosopher has argued that the notion of human rights popularized in the Bill of Rights is an explicitly Christian creation.[10] It would be foolhardy—bordering on delusional—to argue that Christianity was not influential in the creation of our nation. Likewise, I believe the Christian vision of morality given by Jesus in the New Testament is the standard by which all other moral visions ought to be measured (or I would not have written this book).

I do, however, want to push back on the notion that the United States and the church are synonymous. In my part of the world, it's pretty common to see bumper stickers, signs, and even memes that pull the United States, Jesus, and (often) the military together into a confusing mash-up. It's not unusual to see signs featuring a cross draped in an American flag or even Jesus wearing an American flag as a sash. The

10. The heritage and development of the concept of human rights in the wake of the French Revolution and the thought of philosophers such as Locke and Voltaire have been well-documented, but the role of religion, specifically Christianity, is often overlooked in this history. Philosopher Luc Ferry argues that human rights are a direct result of Christianity in *A Brief History of Thought: A Philosophical Guide to Living* (New York: Harper Perennial, 2011).

result of this strain of theology is an odd political posture in which people are convinced that being an American citizen is synonymous with being a Christian. Indeed, the term "evangelical" has changed in its popular meaning directly as a consequence of this blending of Christianity and Americanism. Evangelicals were once defined by their theological beliefs. The Bebbington Quadrilateral is one popular attempt to capture evangelical theological identity, highlighting biblicism (the authority of Scripture), crucicentrism (the centrality of the cross), conversionism, and activism (evangelism and social work in the world).[11] More recently, however, the term "evangelical" has become a political term tied to conservative politics—so much so that many self-labeled evangelicals do not attend church.

I care a great deal about my nation and want the best for it. At the same time, pastors and church leaders must grapple with the fact that more and more Christians—particularly within evangelicalism—see their hope and faith tied as closely to politics as to following Jesus. If we contribute to a mindset of combining the church and our nation, then we can unintentionally convince our congregations that our salvation is found not in Jesus but in who occupies the White House.

If Jesus is no longer the structure to which our ship is moored, cultural currents can toss us about very quickly. Evangelical attitudes toward money, marriage, sexuality, politics, revenge, and any number of topics can shift away from the New Testament more easily when those who self-identify as "evangelical" or even "Christian" spend less time learning from the church and more time learning from the

11. David W. Bebbington, *The Evangelical Quadrilateral: Characterizing the British Gospel Movement* (Waco: Baylor University Press, 2021).

majority culture. Social media, cable news, and YouTube are all too happy to disciple us if we will not allow Jesus to do so.

At some point, the difference between church and culture becomes so minimal that those who are not Christians but are American wonder why Christianity would be something to investigate. If, from their perspective, the church looks like the rest of the culture with an occasional church service, what incentive would they have to join such a church?

When one adds in the increased material prosperity of the West, an almost endless supply of personally tailored entertainment choices offered up via algorithm, a landscape of retail options in every direction, and the rapidly diversifying spirituality of the twenty-first century, the church feels more like something that nice people might choose to do on a Sunday than a community that is distinct from the rest of the world. This is the moment to embrace our difference, to ground our actions and attitudes in the love of God found in Christ, and to allow that difference to be our greatest tool in the renewal of culture. In cultivating a kingdom garden, loving service is the sharpest of trowels.

What better time than now to make the church different?

What better time than now to go back through the looking glass?

That's the object of this book—to remind us of the backward and upside-down values of Jesus and to hold them in tension with our American values. If the church in America is going to move from decline to growth, Christians must become recommitted to knowing and obeying Jesus in a way that will set them apart. The church needs to be distinctive again—like it was in its earliest days.

In short, the American church needs to think less about American values.

Christians need to think about—and be trained in—Jesus's values. Which leads us to treasure hunting.

Jesus was a master storyteller. He was so good, in fact, that he could tell an incredibly compelling story in a sentence or two.

In the Gospel of Matthew, Jesus tells one of those short, powerful stories: "The kingdom of heaven is like treasure, buried in a field, that a man found and reburied. Then in his joy he goes and sells everything he has and buys that field" (13:44).

There is so much *not* told in this story. What was the man doing in the field? Was he looking for treasure? Or did he just stumble upon it? What sort of treasure did he find? Who hid the treasure? Why did that person hide it in the first place?

Jesus skips all those details. They are not important to the story, because the story is about the lengths to which one might go to obtain a treasure. And what did that man do? He "went and sold all he had and bought that field."

The treasure was so valuable that the man gave everything else to get it.

And then, as if Jesus is afraid we will miss the importance of the story about treasure, he immediately tells another very similar story: "Again, the kingdom of heaven is like a merchant in search of fine pearls. When he found one priceless pearl, he went and sold everything he had and bought it" (Matt. 13:45–46).

In the first story, the item of great value is treasure. In the second story, it's an incredibly valuable pearl. In both stories the object is worth giving everything to obtain.

This object, this thing worth giving everything for, is the kingdom of God.

The kingdom (as I'll usually call it) is the focal point of much of the teaching of the New Testament. For the longest time, I assumed that it was shorthand for eternity or heaven or the afterlife with God. But I was wrong. Yes, when Jesus returns to set all things right, he will establish his kingdom in its totality, but that is not how Jesus uses the term throughout the New Testament. And, yes, spending eternity with Jesus is certainly worth giving everything for, but that is not the way Jesus defines kingdom, nor is that the way it is used in the rest of the New Testament.

But the kingdom is incredibly important. It is the focal point of Jesus's first sermon, which was, incidentally, incredibly short: "Repent, because the kingdom of heaven has come near" (Matt. 4:17). Jesus tells story after story to illustrate the kingdom. Over and over he begins a story by saying something like, "The kingdom of heaven is like . . ." After his resurrection, he appears to his disciples and speaks for forty days about—that's right—the kingdom. "He appeared to them over a period of forty days and spoke about the kingdom of God" (Acts 1:3 NIV). If we are to believe that the New Testament reliably speaks about Jesus, that means his first recorded sermon in Matthew was about the kingdom and his final sermon prior to his ascension in Acts was about the kingdom.

For Jesus, things quite literally begin and end with the kingdom.

Not only that, but Jesus seems to indicate that the things of God are best understood by employing the kingdom as our lens of interpretation. Jesus said, "Therefore . . . every teacher of the law who has become a disciple in the kingdom of heaven is like the owner of a house who brings out of his storeroom treasures new and old" (Matt. 13:52). Somehow, according to Jesus, if we become "disciple[s] in the kingdom," we will be able to understand the law of God in a way that is not only tied to the traditions of the past but also fresh and new.

If I understand this verse correctly, it means that if we understand what precisely the kingdom is, we will be able to understand the Bible more fully. Some of the things that never made sense to us will suddenly become clear.

Jesus begins with the kingdom.

Jesus ends with the kingdom.

Jesus tells story after story about the kingdom.

Jesus tells us that we can better understand the Scriptures if we know the kingdom.

If Jesus has one thing that he values, it is the kingdom. It is the thing he considers supremely valuable, the thing he treasures.

If we want to know what Jesus's values are, we should start with the thing he values most—the kingdom.

Jesus's values are found in the kingdom. This is why he commands us to seek the kingdom first (Matt. 6:33). It is the treasure that we should abandon all else to find.

———

If Christians are going to embrace our cultural difference and find the treasure, we will need a map. Every good treasure hunt has one. Our map will guide us through the world in a particular way: through Jesus. Most of the West moves through the world using a different map—one of separation and competition. The majority of Westerners, particularly Americans, believe there is not enough (of most anything), so we must fight with one another to get everything we can. We are tempted to trust a map that leads to a zero-sum outcome.

Such a way of moving through the world makes us increasingly anxious and unsettled.[12]

Jesus, however, tells us that he is the way, the truth, and the life (John 14:6). In my tradition, we have historically taken this to mean that one can get to heaven only through Jesus. (I believe that, by the way.) This verse is much more layered, however. Specifically, Jesus calls himself "the way." His life is not simply an extended passion narrative culminating in the cross; his life is the map for how we ought to live. His way is our way. We ought to live as Jesus lived—not in competition and separation but instead in loving cooperation and collaboration.

In his Pulitzer Prize–winning novel *The Overstory*, Richard Powers introduces readers to a range of characters whose lives eventually intersect around—of all things—trees. One of those characters is Dr. Patricia Westerford, a scientist who discovers that trees talk to one another and share resources through their root systems, which are far more robust than originally believed. After a disastrous response to her findings, she retreats to the forests of the Northwest, where she lives among the trees. One day she comes upon a clearing and has an epiphany: the forest cooperates and collaborates with itself to foster life. Even as things rot, decay, and die, they increase the fertility and fecundity of the forest floor, making things more green, more alive. The goal of living things, she realizes, is to bring about greater flourishing, to foster more life.[13]

12. I am indebted to Jamie Winship for pointing out that there are essentially only two ways of viewing the world.

13. Richard Powers, *The Overstory: A Novel* (Harper: New York, 2019). Westerford is almost certainly based on Dr. Suzanne Simard, whose discoveries about trees are documented in her book *Finding the Mother Tree: Discovering the Wisdom of the Forest* (New York: Knopf, 2021).

Dr. Westerford's realization of how the living things (and even the dead ones) in the forest work together to foster life provides a helpful way to think about creation—as designed to foster life. It also gives us a good way to think about the kingdom and, by extension, Jesus. He is the giver of abundant life (John 10:10). He is the resurrection and the life (John 11:25–26). He gives living water (John 7:37–39). Jesus and life are inseparably intertwined. To choose him is to choose a way of living in the world that cultivates culture through creating life.

The charge to foster life sounds a great deal like the original charge given to humans in the Garden of Eden. There, in Genesis, the first man and woman are charged to tend the garden and to cultivate it. Given the command to have dominion over the earth, humans are introduced into a partnership with God—to make the earth into a place where his vision for life might best be realized. People are to partner with God to bring about greater flourishing. If the kingdom is Jesus's vision to bring about God's will on earth as it is in heaven, it makes sense that the kingdom would be an extension of God's life-giving desire from Genesis. Here is how Blaine Eldredge describes the Garden of Eden: "Heaven and earth overlap, but only in Eden. They're meant to overlap everywhere, until the knowledge of God covers the world like the waters cover the sea. Adam and Eve are assigned to facilitate that union, to structure the world and fill it with life."[14]

I believe that is the kingdom vision for the church.

God's plan for life is one of collaboration and cooperation. Just as Dr. Westerford finally sees how the trees work together

---

14. Blaine Eldredge, *The Paradise King: The Tragic History and Spectacular Future of Everything According to Jesus of Nazareth* (Coppell: Iona Farms, 2023), 33.

to serve one another, the kingdom reflects God's life-giving wish. As we examine Jesus's descriptions of the kingdom, we will see how cooperation and collaboration become more valuable at every turn, surpassing the more traditional Western value of competition.

In the kingdom of God, the citizens see everyone as connected to everyone else. Like the forest promoting life within itself, those in the kingdom see all of humanity connected to one another. Our lives are best lived when we help others live well, when we strive not only for our own flourishing but for the flourishing of everyone. When we live with a collaborative mindset, we begin to understand the way of Jesus, because Jesus desires that all might know his love, that all might experience this way of life.

Abundant life, indeed.

In the 2004 Walt Disney film *National Treasure*, Nicolas Cage plays Benjamin Franklin Gates, a treasure hunter obsessed with finding a legendary treasure belonging to the Knights Templar, Freemasons, and the Founding Fathers. What the film lacks in believability it makes up for in enthusiastic imagination, as clues to finding the treasure are found in the most exotic of locations, including the back of the Declaration of Independence. Gates and his colleagues are mocked and derided by many of the "establishment" players for their reckless abandon to do whatever is necessary to find the treasure. Along the way, Gates and his friends are chased, threatened, and fired on. They concoct a plot to steal the Declaration of Independence. They dig through permafrost to find a shipwreck.

You get the point.

At some point in the film, the clues and the exploits are so ridiculous that Gates's comic-relief sidekick, Riley, quips, "Why can't they just say, 'Go to this place, here's the treasure, spend it wisely'?"

But Riley already knows the answer, as does the audience. Why do he and his friends do all of this? Why go through the trouble of searching for clues and stealing documents? They do these things because they believe there is a treasure with value beyond imagination. As a result, they are willing to do whatever is necessary to obtain this treasure.

Many of us might understand this sort of a treasure hunt, albeit on a much smaller scale. My friend Jason has been searching for an original vinyl pressing of *August and Everything After* by the band Counting Crows for a very long time. He's found a few copies online, but they always cost hundreds of dollars. His treasure hunt is to find an original pressing within a reasonable price range. Personally, I've been on the hunt for a first edition of Dietrich Bonhoeffer's *Cost of Discipleship* (in either English or German) for a very long time. I wrote my doctoral dissertation on Bonhoeffer, so that particular book holds a special place in my heart. So far, no luck. If I found one, I wonder how much money I would be willing to spend to acquire it. Is it a treasure I'm willing to spend everything for? Not quite. But I know I would be willing to spend more on it than any other book I've ever purchased.

While value may have something to do with the eye of the beholder, we can each appreciate hunting for something that is—at least in our eyes—a treasure.

This book is a sort of treasure hunt. Perhaps more accurately, it is me reporting back from my treasure hunt.

In 2008, I heard a presentation on the kingdom of God by Bob Roberts Jr.[15] Pastor Bob's explanation of the kingdom helped me make sense of the New Testament in ways I had never previously been able to do. As a result, I set about reading and rereading the New Testament and books Pastor Bob recommended about the kingdom.

That two-year journey into understanding the kingdom changed my life and the trajectory of my pastoral ministry.

Over the course of this book, I want to tell about the treasure I've found in the kingdom. The kingdom contains the things Jesus finds valuable. I believe that if the American church will seek after these things once again, we will rediscover our difference and, in turn, rediscover what made the church effective in the first place. I believe we will discover how beautiful and powerful it is to see the world as connected and designed for life, how good it is for us to operate from this connection mindset.

Most of the chapters in this book will explore a concept or an issue central to our culture and then hold it up against the things Jesus teaches or says regarding that same issue. Along the way, we will discover Jesus's values and, I believe, better understand the kingdom we are called to embody and seek.

But before we get to those issues, we must consider the kingdom itself. If it is not simply a synonym for heaven or the afterlife, what is it?

15. For a good book on kingdom vision, see Bob Roberts Jr., *Transformation: Discipleship That Turns Lives, Churches, and the World Upside Down* (Grand Rapids: Zondervan, 2010).

2

Heaven Help Us

Imagination and Kingdom Practice

That's just the way things are.
—pretty much everyone

Your will be done on earth as it is in heaven.
—Matthew 6:10

Many of us think about the world in the wrong way. This is not necessarily because we have done anything wrong or because we are uneducated. To the contrary, we have more information now than we have ever had.

But we arrange that information in the wrong way.

Take, for example, the natural world. Many of us have a "red in tooth and claw" understanding of the creation and living things around us. We've watched the nature documentaries of the lion stalking the gazelle, and we have understood the Darwinian implications: the strong prey on the weak; only the fittest survive. This makes sense to us, because that is, after all, the way the world works. The ones who have power tend to use it to benefit themselves, and, furthermore, they use that power to exercise dominion over creatures who are weaker.

We see the strong taking advantage of the weak in almost every arena of life: economics, sports, corporations, organizations, politics, and the like. After a while, we come to accept this as "the way things are."

But is it truly the way things are? Or are they more complex?

Like Richard Powers and his fictional Dr. Westerford from the previous chapter, James Bridle surprises readers in his brilliant book *Ways of Being* with example after example of ways that the natural world is not competing but cooperating—and doing so intelligently. Trees, for example, share nutrients along their root system so that they can all flourish, particularly in times of drought. Trees also communicate with one another through the same root systems (yes, you read that correctly) when they hear the sound of predatory insects or a fire approaching. And, yes, trees are able to "hear." As Bridle notes, when scientists have tried to elicit the same communicative and defensive responses from trees by playing other sounds, the trees do nothing. But if the correct insect sound is played? They work to help their fellow trees.[1]

Yes, there are destructive forces: fires and insects and droughts. But the trees are indeed cooperating. Life is helping life continue; life is helping life flourish.

1. The phrase used to describe this intelligence among trees is the "Wood Wide Web," which I absolutely love. James Bridle, *Ways of Being: Animals, Plants, Machines; The Search for a Planetary Intelligence* (New York: Farrar, Straus and Giroux, 2022).

In August 2017, Houston was ravaged by Hurricane Harvey. Over fifty inches of rain fell on the city in a matter of days. During this crisis, thousands of homes were flooded. And while there were some isolated incidents of looting, the overwhelming response in the wake of the storm was neighborly cooperation. The Cajun Navy from Louisiana's bayous brought their air boats. World Relief sent in supplies. People used canoes and pickups to help their neighbors. I know of an instance where an elderly couple called their local Chick-fil-A—where they ate breakfast each morning. When they couldn't make it because of their house flooding, the Chick-fil-A employees at that particular location dispatched a jet ski to pick them up. (I suppose Chick-fil-A customer service truly is second to none!)

Again, destructive forces are present, but amid the destruction is the beauty of cooperative neighboring.

In some sense, it seems as if the world is torn between two personas, an almost planetary personification of Jekyll and Hyde. On the one hand, parts of the planet are working to destroy and feed on other parts of the same planet. On the other hand, parts of creation are working in concert to help one another in the midst of adverse conditions.

What if "the way things are" is not so singular in meaning? What if "the way things are" points to a world that is torn between ravaging and redemption?

And if that's the case, when we live according to "the way things are," should we live by the notion of cooperation or competition?

There's another way to look at it, of course. What if creation is showing us within itself two options, the way things are and *the way things ought to be*?

Jesus's first sermon was about the way things ought to be. His sermon was short: "Repent, because the kingdom of heaven has come near" (Matt. 4:17). As I discussed in chapter 1, Jesus was not referring to an otherworldly paradise, heaven, or eternity. Rather, he was reviving a concept in Judaism known as *tikkun olam*, sometimes translated as "repair of the world." While *tikkun olam* has had different connotations and uses over the years, the concept is simple enough: We know how things are, but how should things be? By extension, what should I do about it? Where should I turn my trowel to cultivate life in the garden?

We know that there has been a great fall. But human history predates the fall. In Genesis 1, the Lord God puts man and woman in the garden and asks them to cultivate the garden and to have dominion over the earth. There is no sin or corruption, but humanity has been given a unique job—to partner with God in making the world into what it might be. We may think of the Garden of Eden as perfect, but there was tending, cultivating, and other work to do from the beginning. Humans are created to be God's partners in making this world a better place, not simply to wait for the afterlife.

When Jesus preached the kingdom, he was announcing a new way of being in the world—a way focused on living according to how things ought to be, how God wants things to be. He was calling us back to the divine-human partnership forged in Genesis 1.

Shortly after his first sermon, Jesus taught the disciples how to pray. That prayer—commonly known as the Lord's Prayer—teaches us just how central the kingdom was in Jesus's mind:

Our Father in heaven,
hallowed be your name,
your kingdom come,
your will be done,
   on earth as it is in heaven.
Give us today our daily bread.
And forgive us our debts,
   as we also have forgiven our debtors.
And lead us not into temptation,
   but deliver us from the evil one. (Matt. 6:9–13 NIV)

Tucked away between acknowledgment of God's holiness (lines 1 and 2) and permission to pray for our daily needs (line 6), Jesus gives a compact definition of what it means to seek to repair the world.

Your kingdom come, your will be done, on earth as it is in heaven.

Jesus prays for the kingdom to come. And what does it mean for the kingdom to come? Simply put: for God's will to be done on earth as it is in heaven. The kingdom exists anywhere that Jesus is recognized as King or his will is being done.

When Jesus preaches his first sermon, declaring that the kingdom is at hand, he is making a bold pronouncement: The kingdom of God is not something you have to wait on. You can live it right now! You can live in this world as if you were already living in heaven. You can cultivate life wherever you are.

This is what it means to live the kingdom: living in the midst of a world obsessed with "the way things are," yet choosing to live life directed toward "the way things ought to be."

So how ought things to be?

Put differently: How do we know what heaven will be like? What is the life to which we ought to be aiming?

To find our answer, we will look to Jesus and his own answers.

Jesus is the most complete revelation of God given to us. If you want to know what God is like, look at Jesus. As Jesus said, "If you have seen me, you have seen the Father" (John 14:9). This is the miracle of the incarnation. In Jesus, God took on flesh. In the middle of the word "incarnation" you may spy a familiar Latin root—*carne*. If you've ever enjoyed a bowl of chili con carne, you know that carne refers to meat. (My love of Tex-Mex cuisine and theology blissfully collide in this moment.) God made himself known by putting on meat—human flesh—so that we could better understand his character. Jesus is God in meat, God in *carne*. When we read about Jesus in the Gospels, we are reading about the very character and teaching of God. Jesus shows us how God would have us live, because Jesus is God living as a human, indeed as the True Human. Over and against Greek, Roman, and other visions of the divine, God shows us himself in Jesus and invites us to participate in his redemptive work.

To understand the kingdom as Jesus taught and lived it, we must dive into the primary texts that record Jesus's life: the Gospels. While any of the Gospels would give us more than enough source material to examine, most of our discussions will begin with the Sermon on the Mount. Innumerable thinkers and writers over the years have used this sermon as a starting point.[2] It remains the most revolutionary sermon

2. Much has been made over the years with regard to the role of Romans in the continual rebirth of the church and its effect on the likes of Augustine, Martin Luther, John Calvin, and even Karl Barth. While receiving far less

ever preached and, if taken seriously, the most revolutionary text ever envisioned for human existence.

Throughout this book I'll examine topics and concepts that are common points of discussion. Along the way I'll look at "the way things are," taking into account various points of culture. Then I'll look at what Jesus says about those topics, pointing out how his teaching is aimed at the kingdom, at "the way things ought to be."

What if the way things ought to be means that there ought to be widespread cooperation and collaboration among humanity so that we can each live a better life? What if that is an essential part of the kingdom?

We can all look at the world and see things that need to be fixed. We can readily agree that we need assistance with conflict, division, impurity, greed, violence, revenge, and the like. There is no shortage of opinions regarding how to deal with those issues. Politicians and pundits have argued to the point of exhaustion on most any topic we could envision. Philosophers have filled volumes theorizing on how humans might live the good life.

But this is a book about truly living, not about theory. We are embodied creatures. We are not simply brains implanted within cases of flesh. Our minds and our bodies are not separate entities but rather complementary parts of a whole. Bessel van der Kolk's work in psychiatry brought this

---

attention, I find that the Sermon on the Mount has been a similarly formative text for many theologians, creating its own sort of theological tradition. I'm thinking specifically of the earliest Christians, those in the Anabaptist tradition, Dietrich Bonhoeffer, Martin Luther King Jr., Stanley Hauerwas, and Dallas Willard. Despite all their differences, they were all changed by their respective attempts to take the sermon seriously. Perhaps one day the church will finally be able to value Romans and the Sermon on the Mount equally and see how freely the fount of grace in the gospel will fill the cisterns of the kingdom.

concept to the mainstream, but it is not altogether different from the Jewish *nephesh*: humans are not part soul and part body but are rather something made up of both soul and body.[3] Theology cannot simply be a discussion of ideas; it must also tell humans how to live. The best of theology calls us to inhabit our bodies in a particular way, to cultivate the life given in Jesus. As Lore Ferguson Wilbert says, "God wants our whole selves to be engaged in our whole faith. He wants our hearts, hands, heads, feet, minds, emotions—all of it. He is deeply after an integrated relationship with us, bringing all our disparate parts together in our faith practice. There is a very real *action* part of our relationship with Christ that we often push away until all our existential questions, doubts, fears, and concerns are settled."[4]

As we live this counterintuitive theological vision, our bodies teach our minds new ways to think, crafting fresh neural pathways and allowing us to think and love in ways we previously could not have imagined.[5] By living the way of Jesus, we affect our hearts and our minds so that we literally think in new ways. Neuroplasticity becomes a vehicle for spiritual maturity when we learn to live in line with the way God has designed humans to function, thereby allowing us to think in new ways. Consider, for example, how loving our enemies teaches us things about others, which in turn

3. In *The Body Keeps the Score: Brain, Mind, and Body in the Healing of Trauma* (New York: Penguin, 2015), van der Kolk demonstrates conclusively that our bodies cannot be separated from, say, traumatic emotional experiences but must rather have space to process them. This reminded me of the Jewish concept of the *nephesh*.

4. Lore Ferguson Wilbert, *A Curious Faith: The Questions God Asks, We Ask, and We Wish Someone Would Ask Us* (Grand Rapids: Brazos, 2022), 127.

5. Although this is not exactly his argument, I'm thinking here of James K. A. Smith's *Desiring the Kingdom: Worship, Worldview, and Cultural Formation*, Cultural Liturgies 1 (Grand Rapids: Baker Academic, 2009).

makes us think about those same people differently than we did before. As we choose to live the Jesus value of enemy love, we are able to think brand-new thoughts. Living affects our thinking. Living affects our loves.

This is why we must embody our beliefs. Only in doing the things we believe are we changed. Faith may come by hearing, but it grows by doing.

Consequently, I want to explore what it means to make a good-faith attempt at living the way of Jesus, and what it means to embody the kingdom so that we can envision how a faithful church might live. So before we jump into those things Jesus himself values, let's talk about what it will look like for us to seriously embark on the path with Jesus. I suggest the following fundamentals as a place to begin when looking at how we might embody the kingdom: dependence on the Spirit, reliance on community, and imaginative thinking.

―――――

Part of living the kingdom means recognizing that *it requires supernatural help*. As I flesh out the things Jesus discusses and values, it will be easy to consider this a book that provides another set of rules for people to follow, or even to think of following Jesus as one philosophical serving in the cafeteria line of ideas. A life of following Jesus and embodying the kingdom is certainly distinctive, but it must be differentiated from pure philosophy, for living the kingdom is a spiritual endeavor.

Those of us who call ourselves Christians believe that upon our conversion we were given a great gift—the Spirit of God. We are, as the New Testament says, "filled" with the Spirit. The picture given in the Bible is that the very presence of God, who once filled the tabernacle and later the temple, now moves into our beings. When Paul says in 1 Corinthians 6:19–20 that our bodies are temples, he means it quite literally.

The Spirit of God is within us.

And we need it.

We cannot embody the kingdom without the Spirit. The commands of Jesus are impossible to obey on our own. Jesus tells us to love our enemies, to never insult someone, to live generously, to engage in sexual purity, to never hate, to even avoid dark thoughts. I have been a Christian for decades. I have been working to take the commands of Jesus seriously for a large part of my adult life. And I still struggle to live many of the ways Jesus asks of us. When I have been betrayed at a deep level, I have found it difficult to forgive. When I have been afraid of people, I have found it difficult to love. Left to my own devices, I tend toward greed and lust.

This is why, in Galatians 5, Paul tells us that we must live by the Spirit. In verse 16 he writes, "I say, then, walk by the Spirit and you will certainly not carry out the desire of the flesh." The picture he gives is straightforward: once you become a Christian, there are two warring factions within you seeking to control your actions. Paul continues in verse 17: "For the flesh desires what is against the Spirit, and the Spirit desires what is against the flesh; these are opposed to each other, so that you don't do what you want." By "flesh" he means the desires of your heart that are in opposition to the way of Jesus; the flesh is humanity in its natural state. The flesh is changed and overcome by the Spirit. The flesh leads us to predictable and omnipresent outcomes: "Now the works of the flesh are obvious: sexual immorality, moral impurity, promiscuity, idolatry, sorcery, hatreds, strife, jealousy, outbursts of anger, selfish ambitions, dissensions, factions, envy, drunkenness, carousing, and anything similar" (vv. 19–21).

But when I trust and live by the Spirit, a freedom and a power within me takes my life in an entirely different direction. The Spirit, Paul says, allows us to overcome these fleshly desires and outcomes. If we live by the Spirit, he says that we will have completely different outcomes. We will have "love, joy, peace, patience, kindness, goodness, faithfulness, gentleness, and self-control" (Gal. 5:22–23).

This raises a question: If the Spirit is so powerful and transformative, then why is it that so many Christians find themselves following the desires of the flesh instead of the desires of the Spirit?

Martin Luther explained this dynamic in his famous essay "The Bondage of the Will."[6] Apart from faith in Christ, humans are slaves to the flesh. Our decisions are bound to the flesh, and we cannot help but choose to do the fleshly thing. When we come to faith in Christ, our wills are set free by the Spirit, and we are now free to choose the way of the Spirit. It is, however, still a choice. Before we were bound to the flesh. Now we can freely choose between the flesh and the Spirit.

Imagine a jail cell. The door is locked. You cannot leave. This is our life in the flesh. We are bound to bad outcomes. Then one day someone opens the door for us. We are free to leave. Most of us would celebrate and escape our cell immediately. But theoretically, we could choose the cell. Yes, the door is open, but we could choose to stay incarcerated. The Spirit opens the door to our heart, but the Spirit cannot push us into freedom. We must choose to walk by the Spirit.

As you can see, we can fully believe the gospel—that God has done everything necessary for our salvation and redemption in the person of Jesus—and remain in the flesh. We can

---

6. Martin Luther, *The Bondage of the Will*, trans. J. I. Packer (Grand Rapids: Baker Academic, 2012). Luther wrote this essay in 1525.

choose to ignore the call of the Spirit, in part or in full. As we choose to surrender more of our heart's responses to the Spirit, we can obey the difficult commands of Jesus.

But if we do not live by the Spirit, we will fail. And if we have not received the Spirit, we will try to live this supernatural life by sheer self-discipline. This is admirable, and it might lead to some better outcomes, but the life of the kingdom is ultimately spiritual (that is, of the Spirit) and must be pursued as such.

If you're reading this and wondering about how to receive this Spirit, then I have good news: the Spirit comes to all who place faith in Jesus as the Messiah—God's Chosen One who shows us his kingdom. For two thousand years the church has proclaimed a simple message known as the gospel. And if you want the Spirit, you simply choose to believe this message and live it by faith.

The message is this: in the person of Jesus, God has done everything necessary for you to have a relationship with him. By assuming flesh, Jesus showed us that God chose humanity as the target of his redemptive work. Yes, God will redeem all things one day, but humans have a special capacity for relationship with him. By allowing himself to be crucified, Jesus took the penalty for our sin upon his body, providing forgiveness for us. God does not lower his standards for righteousness, but he puts Jesus's righteousness on us in the same moment that Jesus takes our sin. It's a cosmic sin switcheroo. Finally, God the Father raised Jesus from the dead to demonstrate that Jesus is truly his Son, truly the Messiah. The resurrection of Jesus is a promise that one day we too will be resurrected and will live into eternity with Jesus.

If you believe these things—this gospel—then God fills you with his Spirit. And that makes the good news even better news. This life of eternity with God isn't something you have to wait for. You can enjoy it now. You have been loved, so now you freely give that love in obedient partnership with God.

Because once you're filled with the Spirit, you can begin to live this beautiful way of life. You can *choose* to walk in freedom with the Spirit. That is where the kingdom begins. In receiving the gospel message, we can begin living a life of cultivation.

If the internet has a superpower, it's that it connects people with niche interests who once thought they were all alone.

I fell in love with smoked meats when I was a child. Now, thanks to the internet and social media, I follow a host of barbecue craftsmen and craftswomen who make videos on how to—you guessed it—make and find the best barbecue you can imagine. There is a professional community on places like X/Twitter (it's more than arguing . . . sometimes) where I can see what other pastors think or how other churches handle sticky situations. And, of course, the interests are as varied as people. My dad watches YouTube videos about renovating antique tractors. Yes, that's a thing. My mom can find other button collectors. Yes, that's a thing too. My brother can find soccer coaching tips, and my sons find other Star Wars fans. We're in the same family, but we're all interested in different things.

And now we can find others who are interested in the same things in just a few seconds.

Obviously, it's not always beneficial for people with similar interests to find one another. Racists, for example, can find other racist people and groups. But, in many pockets, the internet is used to find some sort of connection across interests that are often broader than our immediate geography.

And, goodness, *there is power in community*. One woman might feel odd dressing up as Iron Man, but if a comic con is in town? She'll fit right in. As the other Avengers come strolling up, flanked by stormtroopers and Klingons, she'll likely feel emboldened. It's often intimidating to do something by ourselves. It becomes less threatening, and even fun, if it's done in a group.

Bottom line: community is powerful. When we are doing what we love with others who love the same things, a sort of "collective effervescence" is formed.[7]

When it comes to living the kingdom, we need this communal, collective effervescence. If we are honest, the commands of Jesus are daunting. Even filled with the power of the Spirit to live them, we will be more emboldened and encouraged if we can jump into the deep end of faith's pool with others who are ready to go swimming with us. When someone else is ready to stand on the edge, hold your hand, and take the plunge, your courage soars. That's how the church works. We encourage one another in doing the good, fending off the foibles of the flesh, and allowing ourselves to be caught in the current of the Spirit.

Community provides more than courage, however. Community provides us with the ability to do something that can make a difference, something that can have influence, something that can be seen. One person acting courageously

7. This is Émile Durkheim's term in his 1912 book *Elementary Forms of Religious Life*, but this experience goes beyond religion. As James Bridle explains in *Ways of Being*, this collective effervescence is experienced in almost any collective activity that brings joy.

can make a difference, to be sure.[8] But when multiple people act courageously in concert, it can bring about very real change. When large groups of people march for civil rights, it can change legislation. As Dr. King and other members of the movement became more organized and gathered more members and momentum, not only were the members of the movement filled with courage, but they were also able to force legal systemic change within the United States.

We also need to live in community so that we can cast a unique vision of how things might be. The Bruderhof—an Anabaptist community—has a slogan that fits this idea: "Another life is possible." When we live the kingdom together in community, we show those outside the church that there is another way to live. We do not have to be driven by possessions, greed, lust, power, or control. We can live lives of love, forgiveness, peacemaking, service, and generosity in such a way that those on the outside cannot help but acknowledge another possibility.

Furthermore, as we live in community, if there are enough of us doing so, we can bring about real change, if only on a small scale. In our church we have adapted the Lord's Prayer as part of our motto: "In Houston as it is in heaven." Using that as our guide, we have found ways to serve those in financial need, welcome refugees, work toward racial reconciliation, help at-risk kids, support first responders, encourage teachers, teach English to immigrants, and any number of smaller acts. I don't know that we have brought significant systemic change to the city of Houston (yet), but we have

8. Dachner Keltner, in *Awe: The New Science of Everyday Wonder and How It Can Transform Your Life* (New York: Penguin, 2023), explains how singular acts of moral courage create awe in the lives of bystanders that surpasses other causes of awe, such as beauty.

absolutely brought change to countless lives through these acts of communal faithfulness.

What happens when community is lived with redemptive cooperation and collaboration in mind so that life might become better for everyone involved? So that life might flourish and become richer?

Kingdom happens.

I know many prognosticators in American Christianity are predicting the sudden collapse of the church in the West. And the American church has enormous problems. But I am convinced that if we can embrace our communal difference from culture at large and live the kingdom in courage and community, then the church has a brand-new opportunity to paint a landscape teeming with life on the canvas of our communities.

But it will require us to think differently. We need imaginative thinking.

Many years ago, Barry Harvey, one of my professors at Baylor University, gave a lecture on the future of the church. He riffed his title from a famous line in the film *Cool Hand Luke*. I've never forgotten it: "What We've Got Here Is a Failure to Imagine."[9]

If the American church has had a failure to imagine, it has been predominantly in how to *be* the church. We have too often focused on production values and "creating

9. If you've never seen it, *Cool Hand Luke* is replete with Christ imagery. It is definitely worth viewing. The line in the movie that Harvey amends to his own purposes is "What we've got here is failure to communicate." For more on imaginative thinking, I highly recommend Barry Harvey, *Taking Hold of the Real: Dietrich Bonhoeffer and the Profound Worldliness of Christianity* (Eugene, OR: Cascade Books, 2015).

experiences" rather than considering how we might faithfully and communally live the kingdom in the public square so that others might see how Jesus can bring life. We need to think about bringing life not only to our churches but also to the communities and neighborhoods where our churches are found. These communities and neighborhoods are, after all, the parish gardens God has charged us to tend. As we seek the betterment of the community, the church will be forced to reconsider the power of the kingdom. One of my mentors, Bob Roberts Jr., puts it this way: "Pastors ask, 'How's my church?' We should be asking, 'How's my city?'"

What might happen if our communal expressions of the kingdom—while focused on living the distinct life of the things Jesus values—extended beyond the walls of the church community and provided healing streams for spiritually parched people? For example, if a church begins focusing on enemy love and reconciliation across dividing lines, how might that spill into our neighbors' homes, schools, streets, and businesses? If we can imagine a way for kingdom living within the community, there *should* be ways for us to imagine how that same way of living might bring vitality and healing into the surrounding community, even if on a small scale.

Roberts says the church can bring healing into the community by carrying the kingdom into the domains of society. As we, for example, love our enemies in a public way in civil society, we become catalysts of community transformation. During the civil rights movement, activists were trained to not engage in violence and instead to look into the eyes of those who screamed racial epithets at them so that the mob would be reminded of the humanity of the activists. Those training the activists knew outcomes would be changed only if hearts were changed. Depending on the timing or audience, the transformation may be small and hyperlocal, but it is important nonetheless. Love transforms much more powerfully than violence.

Part of our current church crisis stems from the fact that we can become too bogged down in what is "realistic" rather than freeing ourselves to think imaginatively once again. If Jesus's hope is for a world in which the Father's will is done on earth as it is in heaven, we should ask some pointed questions. If God's will were happening in our respective communities in a way that reflected heaven, how would that change the following?

- Our finances
- Our daily interactions
- Our workplace
- Communal mental health
- The divorce rate
- Addictions
- Our relationship to politics and power
- The role of service in our hearts

You get the idea. If kingdom became part of our communities, we would see more than churches filling up for worship services. We would also begin to see our cities changed.

The task before the church today, then, is to freely imagine what it might be like if heaven broke into our world. Jesus's arrival was God doing just that—bringing heaven to earth. As Jesus announced the arrival of the kingdom, he was not signifying that heaven had completely taken over the earth, but that the rule and reign of Jesus could now be recognized. The people of Israel may have rejected God as their king in the days of Samuel, but now, through Jesus, they could right that wrong and grab hold of his rulership.

Just as humans were commanded to rule in Genesis, and just as they are promised to rule in Revelation, Jesus invites us to join his kingdom and bring the heavenly vision to earth here and now. If we examine the teachings of Jesus, then we might be able to see the connective tissue between what he taught and what heaven will be like. We can then find the ways to embody heaven today. In doing so, we will bring cooperation and collaboration with God's conception of how humanity ought to live so that we might see life expand and flourish.

That's the goal of this book: to cast a vision for how we can faithfully and communally embody the kingdom way of Jesus in the world by the power of the Spirit and, by doing so, imagine ways that our faithfulness might bring spaces of transformation to our communities.

Jesus's ideas may be radical and difficult, but they remain the best ideas ever uttered. His way may be challenging, but in the end it is the lightest of yokes. It is not a set of rules but rather a stream of living water flowing from the fount of his transformative grace.

So let's turn now to several radical teachings of Jesus and see how we can embody them in a way that could change not only the American church but potentially the communities where we find ourselves. And let's look at each of them through the lens of cooperation and collaboration flowing from God's love for humanity.

3

Power Hungry

Jesus on Humility and Service

So if I, your Lord and Teacher, have washed your feet, you also ought to wash one another's feet. For I have given you an example, that you also should do just as I have done for you.

—John 13:14–15

Life's most persistent and urgent question is, "What are you doing for others?"

—Martin Luther King Jr., Public Address in Montgomery, Alabama (1957)

F rank Herbert's classic science fiction novel *Dune* is a thrilling story of cultural conflict and palace intrigue. It also happens to provide a thoughtful meditation on the juxtaposition of religion and power. *Dune's* protagonist—Paul Atreides—grows up under a prophecy of becoming the Muad'Dib (Messiah) of the Fremen people of the planet Arrakis. Paul believes the prophecy to be simply a myth, but he eventually finds himself thrust into the position of Chosen One for the Fremen people, despite his protests. After coming to power, he faces ethical dilemma after ethical dilemma—specifically, whether or not to engage in a war he knows will result in the death of millions. He finds himself in a position of power over people of faith, and he can control much of their lives simply because they trust him.

Power and faith have an uneasy relationship, particularly in Christianity. I could point to any number of scandals that would illustrate the point. There would be plenty of fodder just in my own denomination. In February of 2019, the *Houston Chronicle* ran an exposé on a number of churches within the Southern Baptist Convention (SBC) and its pattern of covering up the sexual abuse of children.[1] Especially disconcerting was reading story after story of individuals who sexually abused minors and were quietly shuffled off to another church, given an opportunity to "start over" without any sort of consequences. When people of faith trust their leaders, power can easily be abused.

That article became a watershed moment in my life. I'm sure the signs had been there all along, but now I began to see indicators of power hunger within churches everywhere I looked.[2] I saw stories of embezzlement, of abuse, and of dishonesty almost daily in the news. This is not to say that there are not thousands of incredible churches doing incredible work all over the world. At the same time, I began to notice things that I had once missed.

1. Robert Downen, Lise Olsen, and John Tedesco, "Abuse of Faith," *Houston Chronicle*, February 10, 2019.
2. Specifically, "The Rise and Fall of Mars Hill" podcast, the Hillsong scandals, and Katelyn Beaty's book *Celebrities for Jesus* (Grand Rapids: Brazos, 2022) all expose the underbelly of power-hungry church culture.

The stories were so common I began asking questions about our structures: Are churches organized in such a way that they are more susceptible to the abuse of power? We are a people who live by faith. We believe in God. Moreover, we believe that Jesus rose from the dead. It would make sense that Christians would choose to exercise a greater faith in those who are in leadership than members of a typical secular organization.

To make it more complex: Why wouldn't they? Aren't these men and women supposed to be representing Jesus? Shouldn't those who claim to represent the Lord be trustworthy if given power?

Lord Acton coined the well-known cautionary observation that "power tends to corrupt, and absolute power corrupts absolutely." Clearly the church was not exempt from his assessment. Eventually I had to examine myself and the church I pastor. Was there something amiss in *our* structure? In me? Was *I* taking advantage of power and authority that had been given to me by our congregation?

Perhaps most importantly: Is there any way to re-center our churches away from an unhealthy obsession with power? If so, what is it?

Churches aren't the only place where we see the corrosive effects of power. Trust of politicians in our nation is at an all-time low. It's easy to understand why. Those who hold top offices tend to finish their terms far wealthier than when they began—using their position of influence to cash in, quite literally, on insider information to build personal net worth. As I write, Justice Clarence Thomas has come under scrutiny for receiving lavish gifts from billionaire Harlan

Crow for twenty years. Likewise, President Joe Biden's time in office has been tarnished by questionable business deals with Ukraine involving his son Hunter.

There are questions about the deployment of power in almost every area of life, from law enforcement (specifically regarding use of force) to education (specifically regarding the controversial ideas to be discussed on campus). Almost all of us have, in some regard, been on the wrong end of a situation where someone misused their power.

The famous Stanford Prison Experiment of 1971 exposed the problem of power quite clearly. When students were dressed in prison guard uniforms and given power over students dressed like prisoners, they behaved in authoritarian ways that surprised researchers. Likewise, the students who were prisoners began to behave in ways commensurate with real prisoners. If power is given to people, they tend to abuse it, even if they are students at one of the top universities in the nation.[3] Human nature desires a theological vision that lines up with our instincts. This is why many Christians have, historically, looked for ways to avoid taking the Sermon on the Mount and other teachings of Jesus seriously. When, for example, Jesus tells us to love our enemies or to turn the other cheek, we are tempted to explain these commands away. Granted, there may be more context surrounding these commands than we might initially understand (more on that later), but evangelical Christians have a history of pushing these difficult commands toward an imaginary theological ideal rather than something Jesus might want his followers to obey.

3. This experiment is described in detail in Philip Zimbardo, *The Lucifer Effect: Understanding How Good People Turn Evil* (New York: Random House, 2008). While perhaps sensationalized a bit, the book is chilling in its conclusions.

But the kingdom, much like its King, is counterintuitive. And, inexplicably, the counterintuitive turns out to be much better than what we might instinctively believe.

The kingdom qualities of cooperation and collaboration come into play again here. The exercise of power is inherently neither cooperative nor collaborative. While some may argue that those in power can help others with the benevolent extension of life (think of Plato's philosopher-king, for example), there is enough abuse of power to demonstrate that finding a different relationship with power would prove healthier for humanity. Most of those who argue for a closer relationship between the church and the corridors of power, in my opinion, fail to honestly account for the corrosive effects of power on those who hold it for any amount of time, particularly when it comes to abuse of power for personal gain.

As it turns out, Jesus looks at power quite differently than many of us would. As a result, his vision of power is life-giving rather than abusive.

We are all happiness hunting. Every day, we make decisions regarding our lives, relationships, and finances that we believe will result in a greater happiness quotient. Most of those decisions are grounded in what I'll refer to as "self-actualization." By this I mean those things we choose to do in order to obtain the things we want. Self-actualization is when I exercise my own agency to obtain happiness based on my intuitive desires.

If, however, the kingdom and the King are counterintuitive, self-actualization can undermine our happiness. Jesus, in fact, regularly challenges us to live a life that runs against the grain of our instincts. His words continue to challenge us: "If anyone wants to follow after me, let him deny himself, take up his cross daily, and follow me" (Luke 9:23).

We tend to believe self-actualization will bring greater happiness. Jesus says that self-denial will.

In her book *A Philosopher Looks at the Religious Life*, Zena Hitz argues for the long-standing Christian practice of self-abandonment. She does not deny that humans are hunting for happiness. She does, however, argue that the best source of happiness is found in self-denial, not in pursuit of our intuitive desires. In fact, when we sacrifice the thing that we believe to be our intuitive goal, we end up finding a greater happiness granted to us. Hitz writes, "We do not 'grasp' our highest end. Rather, we sacrifice it. In doing so, our happiness is bestowed on us as a prize: it is given, rather than taken."[4]

Our tendency is to chase the things we want with abandon. But Hitz says that in clearing our lives of the very things we think we want, we create space for grace to move more freely. She writes, "Part of the point of renunciation, then, is to clear the obstacles to grace: to break our habits of choosing that blind us to what we might receive."[5] Renunciation and self-abandonment are how we clean out the garden of our hearts in order to make room for kingdom roots to spread. When we choose to remove certain things, we make room for other things. Renunciation gives us the opportunity to plant the things we hope to grow.

I grew up under the tutelage of a plumber. At an early age I learned a simple principle: if you want water to flow, you may have to clear some things out. The human heart operates in

---

4. Zena Hitz, *A Philosopher Looks at the Religious Life* (Cambridge: Cambridge University Press, 2023), 14.

5. Hitz, *A Philosopher Looks at the Religious Life*, 16.

much the same way. When we clear things out, we experience the flow of God within us.

Many of us go through periods of self-denial for our own good. We get off social media; we fast from alcohol; we avoid certain foods; we cut back on television. We know that we need these little tweaks because we can sense our hearts and bodies moving toward atrophy. After a season, most of us return to our former ways. We change, but then we go back to how we were. The Christian life is supposed to be different. It is supposed to be a moment where we move through the looking glass and embrace an entirely new way of being human, where we accept that self-denial is in fact a path to happiness far more satisfying than any hunting we might do in the normal human haunts.

Hitz puts it like this: "The point is not to give up money for a time, to see what it is like; or to fast or to wear a habit for a particular period of penance. It is an attempt to shape one's whole life."[6] Dietrich Bonhoeffer puts it more plainly: "When Christ calls a man, he bids him come and die."[7]

In my years of pastoring, I have found that most people do not truly believe self-denial will bring them greater happiness. Deep down, they often view the choice between following Jesus and following their own desires as akin to choosing between broccoli and a Twinkie. They know that broccoli is better for them, but they do not believe broccoli will make them happier. But what if that isn't the choice at all? What if we are choosing between a Twinkie and chef-prepared bananas foster served over homemade ice cream?

6. Hitz, *A Philosopher Looks at the Religious Life*, 16.
7. Dietrich Bonhoeffer, *The Cost of Discipleship* (New York: Macmillan, 1963), 99.

What if our own desires do produce happiness, but it is a happiness fueled by the spiritual equivalent of partially hydrogenated vegetable oil and number five yellow dye? What if our own desires create a happiness that causes a slow rot that we may not notice for years? And what if choosing the way of Jesus produces a joy that is richer and far more satisfying than we would have ever imagined?

According to Jesus, the call to self-denial will result in greater happiness and satisfaction, no matter what our intuition may tell us. As we clear out the weeds in our lives, we will create a space within our hearts where the living waters of life can flow freely, where grace can water our garden without interference.

Power is the opposite of self-denial. Or perhaps better: seeking unbridled power is the opposite of self-denial. Jesus warned his followers about power: "You know that the rulers of the Gentiles lord it over them, and those in high positions act as tyrants over them. It must not be like that among you" (Matt. 20:25–26). We have all known people who were hungry for power—to be in charge and to lord that power over those under their charge.

At the root, there is a difference between leadership and seeking power.

Someone once told me a rule of leadership that has yet to be disproven in my personal experience: if someone wants to be in charge, they probably shouldn't be. If you've been around the block a time or two—as I have—you've been part of an organization that was poorly run. And you may even have thought or quipped, "I could do a better job than this." But anyone who has ever been in charge—of anything, really—can tell you about all the problems and headaches of leadership. Effective leaders must deal with management issues and organizational headaches that are almost cease-less. The only people who think that leadership is easy are those who have never led.

Anyone with a modicum of leadership experience knows these truths. They know that leadership is difficult and that leading well requires a heart of service.

But those who seek power are not interested in service. They are interested in amassing as much control as possible with as little sacrifice as possible. If self-denial is at the heart of the kingdom, controlling others is anti-kingdom.

The challenge of choosing leadership—instead of control—is one of character. If you lead with integrity, the organization you lead will give you more trust, less oversight, and greater freedom. But when you are granted those hard-earned gifts, the temptation toward leadership entitlement grows larger. Whether it's at the White House or a Waffle House, those in authority can begin to abuse that authority as if they are entitled to it, using power and position to harm those under their charge.

I've heard that the weakest kind of leadership is *positional authority*. Positional authority is authority given because you are above me in an organizational chart or in a hierarchical structure. It is very real authority, particularly if you are my boss. At the same time, it is not a level of leadership that will inspire great action. Similarly, I've heard the strongest kind of leadership is *relational authority*. Relational authority is authority given because of respect. If I respect you and the way you live your life, I will follow you willingly and trust your decisions.

At its simplest level, relational authority outpaces posi-tional authority because relational authority is given by the follower while positional authority is taken by the one in authority.[8]

Jesus was a relational leader. Everywhere he went, people chose to follow him. This was in part because of his teaching. I've long marveled at Matthew 7:28–29: "When Jesus had finished saying these things, the crowds were astonished at his teaching, because he was teaching them like one who had authority, and not like their scribes." Jesus taught as one who had the right to teach about the kingdom of God, not as someone relaying information he had *heard* about the kingdom of God. Jesus had authority because he *knew* the kingdom about which he taught.

Those who hope to be in power seek to be in proximity to it. The king's court is made of those who are close to power and, by extension, can influence decisions. This was the case with Haman and Xerxes, and it is the case with advisers to the president. As Alexander Hamilton brashly sings in the Broadway musical, "I want to be in the room where it happens."[9]

His words describe most of us. There is an aphrodisiac of sorts created in the shadow of power. After all, who wouldn't want to be consulted on the most important of decisions? Who wouldn't want their opinion to be codified?

———

Almost all of us would agree that we want trustworthy leaders in power—people who will lead with integrity and

8. Relational authority, it must be said, can absolutely be abused. Many narcissists and manipulators have convinced people to follow them, only to then use their authority and influence in destructive ways. My point here is not that relational authority is perfect but that relational authority is stronger because it is given rather than taken. Healthy relational authority will always outpace positional authority.

9. *Hamilton: An American Musical*, music and lyrics by Lin-Manuel Miranda (2015).

honor. We want people who will do their best to guide us, to craft policies, to lead our institutions. We know that leaders are necessary for the world to run well. At the same time, we recognize just how rare it is to find good leaders.

We need a way of thinking about influence that is not obsessed with control.

This is the brilliance of Jesus. He was granted relational authority by those around him, but he never attempted to control those in his circle. Those who followed him chose to do so. He would call, and they would answer—or not. Some followed him for a time and then stopped doing so. The Gospel writers never speak of Jesus attempting to convince his followers to stay, but they regularly mention him saying things so difficult that they baffled hearers.[10] Jesus gave his disciples a real choice to follow and a real choice to leave. He had authority, but he did not abuse it.

The people marveled at Jesus, however, not just because of his teaching but because he loved them. Jesus welcomed children. Children were not respected in the ancient world; they were a liability in many cases. Jesus embraced them and blessed them. He also honored, conversed with, and blessed women. He loved women in a way that made them feel comfortable being his disciples and in a way that flouted cultural norms. He did not threaten women; he respected them. Jesus approached the sick, the lame, the blind, and the weak. Rather than running from those who might be seen as a burden or a time waster, Jesus went to them. Jesus listened to them. He touched them. Jesus sat with the outcast sinners. He allowed prostitutes to wash

10. I suppose John 6:67 might be an exception to Jesus never actively asking his disciples to stay: "So Jesus said to the Twelve, 'You don't want to go away too, do you?'" This, however, is not clear, so I stand by the point.

his feet and ate dinner with embezzlers. His love was indiscriminate.

Love was the defining characteristic of Jesus's leadership. Love is the difference between leadership and control. Love is the difference between positional and relational authority. Love is the way power can be redeemed.

And the public demonstration of love is *service*.

Most of the conversation in evangelical circles regarding power involves institutions: universities, governments, and the like.[11] The questions of institutions is an important one and should be given a great deal of energy. I, however, am less concerned in this chapter with strengthening institutions and more concerned with the faithful witness of the church. And I am convinced that the most influential thing most churches and pastors could do today is to serve their neighbors. Too many of our pastors sound like pundits. Too few of us wash feet.

Jesus's final act of teaching before sharing a meal with his disciples and then journeying to the cross was an act of joyful service. Taking the position of a household servant, he washed the filthy feet of grown men—toenails and all. He knew he would soon be in excruciating pain, bound to endure death and the grave. And yet he taught his disciples that the most important thing to do was to serve.

He said as much to them as he finished: "So if I, your Lord and Teacher, have washed your feet, you also ought to wash one another's feet. For I have given you an example, that you also should do just as I have done for you" (John 13:14–15).

11. I find Andy Crouch, *Strong and Weak: Embracing a Life of Love, Risk, and True Flourishing* (Downers Grove, IL: IVP Books, 2016) and Adam Kahane, *Power and Love: A Theory and Practice of Social Change* (San Francisco: Berrett-Koehler, 2010) to both be very helpful in thinking through a theology of institutions.

Earlier I referenced Matthew 20:25–26: "Jesus called them over and said, 'You know that the rulers of the Gentiles lord it over them, and those in high positions act as tyrants over them. It must not be like that among you." Jesus is clear that we are not supposed to lord our power over others. But what *are* we to do?

Verses 26–28 make it plain: "On the contrary, whoever wants to become great among you must be your servant, and whoever wants to be first among you must be your slave; just as the Son of Man did not come to be served, but to serve, and to give his life as a ransom for many."

Whoever wants to be great among you must be your servant.

Jesus says it clearly. If you want to be considered great among your community, do not seek power or control. Don't pursue political influence. Don't focus on obtaining power.

If you want to be great in your community, you must serve.

This is the line of action churches ought to pursue.

We struggle to serve. I can only assume it is because most of us believe Jesus is mistaken or naive.

But if we believe that Jesus truly is God incarnate, then he is not mistaken. He is, as Dallas Willard said, the smartest person to have ever lived.[12] And if the smartest person to have ever lived tells me that the best way to achieve cultural influence is to serve others, then I want to take him at his word. I want to think of ways to serve our community, because serving builds trust (the foundation of relational authority) and is a practice of self-denial (the foundation of the kingdom). When we serve our neighbors without expecting something in return, we model Jesus. We show his love, which is freely given, whether others choose to respond or not. Service is the embodiment of the gospel.

12. Dallas Willard, "Jesus the Logician," *Christian Scholar's Review* 28, no. 4 (1999): 605–14.

We do not change hearts by packing the Supreme Court, boycotting a specific business, or supporting a specific politician. Those tactics may change laws or businesses, and they may help craft a better world in which to live, but they will not change hearts. Human hearts are changed by love, particularly divine love. The smartest man to have ever lived—Jesus—knew this. This is why he told us to serve. When we serve others without an expectation of reciprocity, return, or quid pro quo, we demonstrate the heart of God.

As I mentioned earlier, Houston was flooded by Hurricane Harvey in 2017. The flooding was devastating. Fifty-one inches of rain fell across our area—enough to literally indent the earth's crust in the Houston area by two centimeters.[13] Oh, and our church's campus was flooded. We had never flooded before, but this flooding was significant. Several feet of water stood in our buildings. By the time the water receded, enormous damage had been done. Our Children's Building had structural damage and would no longer be safe for use. It was effectively condemned, and we had to tear it down.[14]

It is difficult to describe the devastation unleashed on the neighborhood around our church's property. Every single home was flooded. Boats went up and down streets, rescuing people from roofs, balconies, and windows. One man in our

13. Alexis C. Madrigal, "The Houston Flooding Pushed the Earth's Crust Down 2 Centimeters," *The Atlantic*, September 5, 2017, https://www.theatlantic.com/technology/archive/2017/09/hurricane-harvey-deformed-the-earths-crust-around-houston/538866/.
14. Our Children's Building was the first building our church ever owned. It was built (at least partially) by volunteers in the 1970s and contained a beautiful chapel. Sadly, the wood-frame construction could not withstand the floodwaters. Thankfully, the rest of our church's facilities employed metal beams.

congregation was rowing a canoe down a major thoroughfare and felt his paddle hit something. He looked underneath his canoe and saw the top of a pickup truck. The water was that deep.

As the floodwaters receded, our church—like many churches in the area—sprang into action. We began "mudding out" (also called "mucking out") the homes of our neighbors. Mudding out a home is not complex, but it is not easy, either. To mud out a home, a crew of people work to mitigate any potential mold that might grow so that the house can remain habitable. First, all carpet is removed and hauled to the curb, and all walls are removed below the floodwater line, being taken down to the studs. All water is pushed outside. Fans are positioned to dry out the house. The house is then thoroughly scrubbed with a solution containing bleach or other cleaners to prevent black mold from growing. Once the house has dried out, renovation can begin.

I have no idea how many houses our church mudded out or helped mud out. The number is easily in the hundreds. Maybe we crossed into the thousands. It was almost all we did, day and night, for two months.

Early in the flood recovery process, we made a decision: we would have a small crew stay behind to work on our church's facilities, but we would send the lion's share of our church into the community to serve our neighbors. To be honest, we didn't think long about the decision. It seemed obvious. The needs in the neighborhood were so massive we knew we had to help.

But the neighborhood noticed. People would stop me as we walked down the street from house to house and thank me for our church's serving without expecting payment. (Turns out professionals were charging a hefty sum for mudding out homes.) Many people who had no intention of attending our church donated to our relief efforts because they saw our work.

Perhaps my favorite story happened when one of the men in our church went to the grocery store and saw a Muslim woman in her hijab purchasing supplies he knew meant her family had most likely been flooded. He approached her.

"Excuse me," he said, "but I noticed what you are buying, and I wanted to see if your family needed any help mudding out your house."

"Oh! Thank you," she replied, "but a group of Christians from a church called Houston Northwest [that's our church] have already helped us. They did everything! I think if people knew that this was how Christians acted, everyone would want to be a Christian!"

I think she's right.

And I think this was why Jesus emphasized service and humility repeatedly. He knew that our tendency would be to grasp for power. But he also knew that loving service would have far greater influence.

Bob Roberts Jr. has more global influence than any other pastor I know. He has met with multiple presidents and kings around the world. How did this happen? Through service. He once told me, "There are two ways to stand before a king. One way is because you know someone who is friends with the king. The other way—the better way—is because the king hears about something you are doing to help his subjects and asks to meet you."

That sounds like the Jesus principle of service in practice. When we mud out houses, feed the hungry, provide counseling, help addicts, pick up trash after the annual Independence Day parade, help the homeless, provide meals for the elderly, or do any number of things that make sense in our communities, we model the very things that Jesus values. As it turns out, these are also the sorts of things that make kings curious enough to inquire after you.

When we chose to serve our neighbors during Hurricane Harvey, we were not seeking notoriety. Yet we received it. I was interviewed by newspapers, local television, and even a national broadcast. We became connected with like-minded churches serving in the city and joined local efforts to help our city on all sorts of fronts, from food insecurity to education. I was soon invited to a multifaith meeting with the chief of police to discuss the best way to help the mental health of law enforcement officers in our city. I did not seek this invitation; it was offered because our church had a reputation of serving our community. I tell this story not to draw attention to me or to our church but rather so that you can understand how I personally discovered the surprising power of service. I wasn't standing before a king, but Bob's principle made more sense now. The more you serve, the more influence you gain. You don't have to elbow your way in; you are invited.

Jesus knew what he was talking about.

When we do this, people see the true heart of God. Service is, in essence, a form of prophecy. Rather than obsessing over the halls of power, we serve those in need, trusting that our works are one of the ways we might speak truth to power. When we prophesy through service, we gain cultural influence that lasts longer than we might imagine, because we change hearts.

Where the unhealthy exercise of power takes away agency and flourishing, serving allows us to share our lives so that we might extend the kingdom all around.

As World War II was drawing to a close, Dietrich Bonhoeffer penned a sermon for the occasion of his nephew's baptism. Bonhoeffer's mood is reflective as he writes and considers the future of the German church that has so fully identified with the Nazis. He knows that the church will soon be without any credibility, and he considers how it might regain that credibility once again. He writes, "Our church has been fighting during these years only for its self-preservation, as if that were an end in itself. It has become incapable of bringing the word of reconciliation and redemption to humankind and to the world. So the words we used before must lose their power, be silenced, and *we can be Christians today in only two ways, through prayer and doing justice among human beings.*"[15] Bonhoeffer intuited the way forward for the German church, the American church, and for any church. We must live from the spiritual (prayer), and we must serve in the physical. When we serve, we model Jesus. Then, and only then, do we further the kingdom.

Jesus, our King, said the kingdom best advances through service. He lived that service by willingly embracing the cross. What if we were to stop fighting for the self-preservation of the church as an end in itself and instead witness to the kingdom of Jesus by embodying prayer and service among our community? I suspect the kingdom would grow, just probably not in the ways we expect.

Washing feet is not weak. Jesus—and Bonhoeffer—knew better.

Serving is where strength begins.

---

15. Dietrich Bonhoeffer, *Letters and Papers from Prison*, vol. 8 of Dietrich Bonhoeffer Works, ed. Christian Gremmels, Eberhard Bethge, and Renate Bethge, trans. Isabel Best, Lisa Dahill, Reinhard Krauss, and Nancy Lukens (Minneapolis: Fortress, 1998), 389 (emphasis added). Earlier English editions translate "doing justice among human beings" as "righteous acts before men."

4

There Is No Them

Jesus on Enemy Love

But I tell you, love your enemies and pray for those who persecute you, so that you may be children of your Father in heaven.

—Matthew 5:44–45

If you love your enemies, you will discover that at the very root of love is the power of redemption.

—Martin Luther King Jr., from his sermon, "Loving Your Enemies"

Several years ago I traveled to Israel and the West Bank. As part of the trip, I visited a place called Tent of Nations. The Tent of Nations is a farm belonging to the family of Daoud Nassar, dating back to the Ottoman Empire. For over a hundred years, family members have tended olive trees, wheat, grapes, and other crops.

The Nassar farm is unique, however, in that it is surrounded by five Israeli settlements. These Israeli settlers believe the Nassar family land is divinely appointed for Israel. As a result, they continually employ intimidation and attacks in an attempt to make the Nassar family surrender their property and move. Bulldozers have destroyed olive trees; vandals have set fire to the farm; masked attackers have physically assaulted family members. Daoud estimates over 150,000 euros' worth of damage has been done to the farm over the years.[1]

And yet, at the entry to the family farm, Daoud and his family posted a sign explaining why they will not retaliate against their attackers. It simply reads:

We Refuse to Be Enemies.

My meeting with Daoud was a transformative moment. I knew Jesus taught his followers to love their enemies, but I failed to grasp the concept until this moment. There, standing in a cave on the Nassar farm, seeking shade from the sun, I slowly began to understand what may be the most radical command Jesus ever gave:

Love your enemies.

Revenge is intuitive.

We desperately want people to get what they deserve, particularly those who have wronged us. Such vengeance is portrayed in stories ranging from *The Count of Monte Cristo* to *The*

1. You can read more about Tent of Nations and the Nassar family at www .tentofnations.com.

Shawshank Redemption to Batman. When I was a young boy, I often fought with my brother in order to administer what I believed to be a reasonable justice. When I became a father, I often saw my own sons attempt to do the same thing. If I'm honest, I still feel my need for justice bubble up when someone attempts to cut in front of me in a line or drive on the shoulder of the road to pass stalled traffic. (Some of us allegedly pull halfway onto the shoulder in order to prevent people from passing. Allegedly.)

Each of us yearns for justice. And each of us, if we live long enough, will experience some form of denied justice. These can range from the frustratingly banal, like not receiving a proper refund or attention in a difficult customer service incident, to the truly tragic, like seeing a known child molester walk free because of a mistake in legal proceedings. I am old enough to have experienced both ends of the spectrum of denied justice and many points in between.

There is something within humans that grows angry at denied justice. In many cases this is a righteous anger. When the molester walks free because of a procedural error, how can you help feeling anger? Why would the guilty walk free? Why would a child be forced to face this abuser time and again? These sorts of injustices happen to us and around us each and every day.

Then there are larger, categorical injustices. When I see prejudice and racism, my anger flares righteously. When I see people grow wealthy at the expense of the poor, that same righteous anger rises. When I watch religious charlatans lining their pockets through the misrepresentation of Jesus, that same anger flares.

And yet, no matter how mad I get, I am rarely able to solve any of these injustices.

Which is what leads me to revenge.

Batman is such an enduring character, at least in part, because his desire to fight crime in Gotham City came from the murder of his parents by a mugger.[2] Each time Bruce Wayne becomes Batman, he embodies a form of vigilante justice inspired by revenge. Every time Batman foils a criminal plot, there is something happening beyond the truth, justice, and American way of Superman. This is not simply about ideology or morality. Batman is, on some level, out for blood.

And we love it.

If you're at all like me, then I imagine you too have yearned for revenge. I imagine you have been hurt, betrayed, abandoned, or forgotten.

And someone has to pay.

This is the great paradox: we are commanded to love our enemies, and yet we deeply yearn for justice. I would go so far as to say that we cannot love our enemies if there is no justice. This is one of the reasons for the cross.

Enemy love is rooted not only in the teachings of Jesus but also in the cross. The cross may be the most radical interpretation of kingdom cooperation possible.

As Jesus sat down on a hillside overlooking the Sea of Galilee, he knew his audience well. Most if not all of his hearers were Jewish, and they were well acquainted with the iron-fisted rule of Rome. The Romans were exacting in taxes and swift in meting out justice—much of which was violent. The people did not like them, to put it mildly. Jesus was looking into the eyes of people who had enemies—not

2. For the comic book enthusiasts such as myself: I'm obviously thinking here of the more recent iterations of Batman, particularly as imagined by DC Comics and filmmaker Tim Burton in the 1990s and then reinvigorated by filmmakers Christopher Nolan and, most recently, Matt Reeves.

theoretical enemies, but real live enemies who were militarily occupying their homeland, taxing them, and building up pagan worship.

You can understand why the wisdom of the day would have been to "love your neighbor," as the Torah commanded, but why the follow-up advice would have been to "hate your enemy." Like any hopeful revolutionaries, the people knew who to trust and who to despise.

Jesus, then, confounds his audience when he says, "You have heard that it was said, Love your neighbor and hate your enemy. But I tell you, love your enemies and pray for those who persecute you, so that you may be children of your Father in heaven" (Matt. 5:43–45). Jesus says that to love your enemies, to pray for those who are persecuting you—those are the marks of those who belong to God. Those who do these things are children of God.

At the end of his life, as he hangs on the cross, Jesus does what he has commanded his followers to do: he prays for his persecutors. "Father, forgive them, because they do not know what they are doing" (Luke 23:34). In the very same verse, his executioners cast lots to divide up his clothes.

As they fight over his garments, as he bleeds and sweats and cries, the God-man from Nazareth, this itinerant rabbi who taught around Galilee, demonstrates his divine patronage by praying for his killers.

Father, forgive them.

We are confronted with questions: How could he do such a thing? How could he pray for those who were in the process of killing him? And how could he expect us to pray for our enemies? We may not face literal killers (then again, some of us may), but his example is so stark we cannot help but wonder how we might ever live up to such a vision of love.

The earliest Christians certainly took the command to heart. The early church quoted the command to love enemies repeatedly. As Preston Sprinkle notes, "Jesus' command to 'love your enemies' was the most popular verse in the early church. It was quoted in twenty-six places by ten different writers in the first three hundred years of Christianity, which makes it the most celebrated command among the first Christians. Matthew 5:44 was the so-called John 3:16 of the early church."[3]

So powerful was Jesus's example that when the first-ever Christian martyr, Stephen, was stoned for his faith, he prayed something almost identical to Jesus: "Lord, do not hold this sin against them!" (Acts 7:60).

What drove this insistence on loving enemies? No other religion has such a command.

The answer is found in the Christian theology of the cross.

In his letters to early churches, the apostle Paul describes Christians as people who were once enemies of God: "You once were alienated and hostile in your minds as expressed in your evil actions" (Col. 1:21). He puts it even more plainly in Romans 5:10: "We were enemies," he says of our relationship with God. These truths apply equally to Christians today because of our sinfulness, our rebelliousness, and our desire to please self rather than God.

God, however, does not choose to smite his enemies. Rather than wiping us out, God chose to become flesh and die on our behalf. The miracle of the cross is not a simple "Jesus died for our sins," however true that may be. Instead, the shocking news of the cross is that God demonstrated enemy love to the highest degree. Those who would have been cast out are brought to the Supper table. Rather than banishment, a

---

3. Preston Sprinkle, "Love Your . . . Enemies?," Theology in the Raw, August 13, 2016, https://theologyintheraw.com/love-your-enemies/.

banquet is set before us. The banner God waves going into battle is not the traditional banner of tribal name, but it is instead the banner of love. God will do whatever is necessary to set a place for us next to him, to bring us into his love. This is how he makes life within us: he loves us like we have never been loved before. He fights for us with love. He will not only wash our feet like a common servant; the God-man will even die for us. There are no lengths to which God will not go to track down those once considered unclean, those once considered too far gone for the religious. Religion dies at the cross and becomes radical love. Enemies become family.

The cross is the object lesson for the church in the radical command of enemy love, because Jesus dies for his enemies. Justice for sinfulness is meted out on the cross. If anyone has confessed and repented, then those sins are hung on the tree with the mangled body of Jesus. The penalty for sin is satisfied, as Romans 5:9 says, having been "justified by his blood."

But what of those sins that are not confessed? What of those injustices that are not righted at the cross?

The perpetrator of a great injustice against me can confess and repent of that injustice, and his wrongdoing will be set right at the cross because his sinful injustice is placed on Jesus's body. But what of those injustices never confessed? What of those injustices held like a knife against our throats our entire lives, injustices that cut us when we try to maneuver away from their hold on us?

According to the Christian story, those injustices will be dealt with when Jesus returns to set things right. In those last days Jesus will make all things new, and every tear will be wiped away. The great biblical book of apocalyptic literature, Revelation, reminds us that Death itself and even Hades will one day be destroyed. The return of Jesus is the death of Death. And on that day all injustices will be set right. All the things we have carried in our bodies, all our traumas, all our anger will finally be released, because the judgment of God will be completed.

That which was not paid for at the cross will finally be purged.

Those who follow Jesus must hold fast to these thoughts. When vengeance clouds our desires, we can rest in the fact that the things that have wounded us either have already been forgiven at the cross or will one day be judged by the King.

Paul, I think, had this theological framework in mind when he penned his letter to the Romans. There he reminds those believers living in the belly of the pagan beast—Rome—to tamp down any desire they may have to strike back at the rulers of the day from a position of vengeance. He writes, "Friends, do not avenge yourselves; instead, leave room for God's wrath, because it is written, Vengeance belongs to me; I will repay, says the Lord" (Rom. 12:19).

Paul instructs them to do the very thing that Jesus told them to do instead of striking back: love their enemies. He continues: "If your enemy is hungry, feed him. If he is thirsty, give him something to drink. For in so doing you will be heaping fiery coals on his head" (Rom. 12:20, alluding to Prov. 25:21–22).

For years I believed Paul was instructing enemy love so that enemies would be made to feel guilty. If you give your enemy food and drink, I thought, then they will feel guilty, and it will be as if they have burning coals on top of their heads. But sometime later I heard a completely different interpretation.

Each household maintained a fire for cooking and warmth. The fire was essential to the operation of the household. If a house's fire went out, they were unable to cook or to stay warm. When this happened, people would go out with a large platter—carried on top of the head—and ask for coals from a neighboring household's fire. In providing these coals, the neighbor helped reignite the fire of their friend in need.[4]

In feeding an enemy, you are not shaming the person into right action; you are loving the person into peace. When I love my enemy in the spirit of the cross, I embody the sign found at the gate of the Tent of Nations, with its refusal to be enemies.

True transformation takes place when a community of believers chooses to live out this value corporately. Each of us can likely imagine someone who is our *personal* enemy, and we may be able to envision what it might look like to love them individually. The more difficult task—and the more powerful force—is when a congregation chooses to love those who want to destroy them. The Black church in the United States has been my best teacher on this front. In the face of church bombings and burnings, anger and animosity, their primary witness has been one of forgiveness, love, and service.

If the earliest Christians were marked primarily by their faithfulness to enemy love, what might that look like today?

In 2011, after the New Year's Day bombing of a church in Alexandria, Egypt, protests and violence broke out across Cairo. Many Muslims gathered in the city center to pray as a form of protest. Photos soon emerged of Christians circling the praying Muslims, holding hands, protecting them from violent protestors. The photos went viral on social media and were soon published by media outlets as a stunning example of unity.

I once heard about church members who showed up on a Sunday morning and found protestors on their campus. After some discussion, the congregation decided to bring coffee

---

· 4. Mazhar Mallouhi shared this insight with me during a conversation in Orlando in 2016. I think the spirit of the interpretation fits with the New Testament's command of enemy love.

and breakfast to the protestors—essentially defusing what might have been a dangerous situation. While this conflict was not nearly as explosive as the situation in Egypt, both examples show us how we might exemplify enemy love in an effort to cultivate the kingdom.

When we serve and love our enemies in community, we refuse to accept the wider culture's talking points and instead provide a new perspective on how to handle conflict. We may pray faithfully for the leaders and politicians who we believe are most opposed to our way. After all, Jesus told us to pray for those who persecute us. We may openly serve those who heap hatred on us. When we wash the feet of our enemies, we confuse them, puzzling them into reconsidering their hatred for us. To be fair, our love may be perceived as weakness, and we may be treated as a soft target, met with hatred and violence. Loving enemies does not always end with a peaceful resolution.

But when we choose enemy love, we find a way forward, discovering the way of Jesus.

In the American context, the most powerful voices teaching enemy love come from the Black church tradition. During the civil rights era, several Black pastors rose to prominence, but none became more influential than Martin Luther King Jr. In his little book *A Gift of Love*, chapter after chapter explains the power of enemy love—made all the more poignant when you consider the circumstances from which King wrote. Even as he faced death threats, vitriol, and the Klan, King spoke openly and courageously about the redemptive power of enemy love.

"Love is the only force capable of transforming an enemy into a friend. We never get rid of an enemy by meeting hate with hate; we get rid of an enemy by getting rid of enmity. By its very nature, hate destroys and tears down; by its very nature, love creates and builds up. Love transforms with redemptive power."[5]

That sounds a lot like heaping coals on the head of our enemy. Only by loving your enemy can you ever change the relationship.

In a 1957 sermon at Dexter Avenue Baptist Church, King said something quite similar from the pulpit:

> Now there is a final reason I think that Jesus says, "Love your enemies." It is this: that love has within it a redemptive power. And there is a power there that eventually transforms individuals. That's why Jesus says, "Love your enemies." Because if you hate your enemies, you have no way to redeem and to transform your enemies. But if you love your enemies, you will discover that at the very root of love is the power of redemption. You just keep loving people and keep loving them, even though they're mistreating you. Here's the person who is a neighbor, and this person is doing something wrong to you and all of that. Just keep being friendly to that person. Keep loving them. Don't do anything to embarrass them. Just keep loving them, and they can't stand it too long. Oh, they react in many ways in the beginning. They react with bitterness because they're mad because you love them like that. They react with guilt feelings, and sometimes they'll hate you a little more at that transition period, but just keep loving them. And by the power of your love they will break down under the load.[6]

5. Martin Luther King Jr., *A Gift of Love* (New York: Penguin Random House, 2017), 50–51.

6. Martin Luther King Jr., "Loving Your Enemies," sermon delivered at Dexter Avenue Baptist Church in Montgomery, Alabama, on November 17, 1957 (approximate date). According to the King Institute at Stanford University, King also worked on a version of this sermon for the *Journal of Religious Thought*; the reprint did not appear until 1970 (*Journal of Religious Thought* 27 [Summer Supplement 1970]: 31–41). This sermon can be accessed

Clearly, King believed enemy love was the only way to transform enemies into friends. When we treat enemies as enemies, we perpetuate the cycle of violence and hatred. But when the church chooses enemy love in the way of Jesus, we break the cycle and create a new pathway. Vengeance rarely ends where we think it will, anyway. We tend to think that if we get vengeance, we will feel better, but when we do get vengeance, we discover that it isn't enough. Like sneaking a second slice of pie, vengeance itself does not satiate; it makes us sick. Our bloodthirst is quenched only when we have practically drowned ourselves in the fount of revenge.

Another giant of the civil rights era, John Perkins, puts it like this: "To choose forgiveness requires that we fight back our human desire for revenge. Revenge is dangerous because it's never really satisfied with an eye for an eye. Instead it rushes quickly into 'punitive excess' taking much more from the offender than is due."[7]

Revenge never satisfies, because revenge does not satisfy our need for true justice. True justice is found only in the cross and at the hand of an all-righteous King.

This is why we are moved when an Amish community forgives the one who kills five students in a one-room schoolhouse in Lancaster, Pennsylvania. This is why we are stunned when an African American church forgives a shooter who kills nine people in a Bible study.

Forgiveness is the path to enemy love. Enemy love is the only path for enemies to be redeemed, to become neighbors. Therefore, enemy love is the only path for peacemaking.

---

at https://kinginstitute.stanford.edu/king-papers/documents/loving-your-enemies-sermon-delivered-dexter-avenue-baptist-church.

7. John Perkins, *One Blood: Parting Words to the Church on Race* (Chicago: Moody, 2018), 107.

In 1219, at the height of the Crusades, many Christians believed that the only way to defeat Islam was to eradicate it on the battlefield. Saint Francis, however, had a different vision. In the midst of battle, Francis crossed enemy lines and received an audience with Malik al-Kamil, the sultan of Egypt. He shared a vision of peace instead of war and proposed that his Order of Friars live peaceably in the midst of Muslims. Stunningly, it worked, and peace came.[8] Saint Francis is most well known as a patron saint of animals to many Western Christians,[9] but his greatest legacy is that of a communal leader of peacemaking in the face of death. This is the way peacemaking happens—risking life to propose peace. What possibilities might open before the American church if we would be willing to model such behaviors toward our enemies?

Tied to Jesus's radical command of enemy love is one of the Beatitudes mentioned early in the Sermon on the Mount. In Matthew 5:9 Jesus says, "Blessed are the peacemakers, for they will be called sons of God." In both the command to love enemies and in the peacemaking beatitude, the divine family is invoked. Those who are peacemakers are sons of God. Those who love enemies show themselves to be children of the Father. Jesus does both. He is a peacemaker and a lover of enemies. While Christians already believe him to be the Son of God, his actions as a peacemaker and a lover of enemies only verify his status as such.

8. Paul Moses tells this story beautifully in *The Saint and the Sultan: The Crusades, Islam, and Francis of Assisi's Mission of Peace* (New York: Penguin Random House, 2009).
9. Many churches today hold services where they bless animals in honor of Saint Francis.

If we aspire to live this Jesus way, then, how do we extend from loving our enemies to actively seeking peace?

Biblical peace—*shalom*—is more than simply the absence of conflict. It is flourishing. Jesus says that those who work to create a holy flourishing for people are acting as if they are in God's family. Peacemaking is not passive. It is, in fact, making something. When we hear of military peacekeepers on the ground in former conflict zones, they are policing an area of high tension, simply attempting to maintain a cease-fire. This is not peacemaking.

Peacemaking is more than keeping warring factions on opposite sides of the street. Peacemaking is bringing warring factions to a place where they understand one another and—while they may never agree—learn to live together in a way where both can flourish. Peacemaking often means that those standing between the warring factions will be maligned and attacked, because peacemakers will ask those who are enemies to see one another's humanity. Peacemakers can take hits from opposing sides, often becoming a sort of peace offering in the process of attempting to make peace. This is what Jesus did. This is, it seems, the way to cultivate life, by laying down one's own preferences in order to make way for greater life.

The cross is not only the picture of God's willingness to love enemies. The cross is also the picture of God's desire to bring all things to their intended state. All things will be made new, and somehow all things pass through the redemptive sacrifice of the cross. As Colossians 1:19–20 says,

> For God was pleased to have
> all his fullness dwell in him [the Son],
> and through him to reconcile
> everything to himself,

whether things on earth or things in heaven,
by making peace
through his blood, shed on the cross.

The blood of Jesus does not only forgive the confessed injustices of our transgressors. The blood also makes a way for him to make all things new, to bring a bruised creation into the eternal weight of glory.

The cross is God's commitment to peacemaking.

What does that mean for us? How do we as God's people live a cross-shaped peace in the midst of a conflict-riddled culture?

In the days after 9/11, I learned a great deal about Islam. Or, rather, I should say that I learned a great deal of incorrect information about Islam. I was not alone. Christians across our nation were learning about Islam from untested sources, many of whom turned out to be wrong. Others, sadly, turned out to be con artists.[10] Politics often employs fear as currency, so it is not surprising that much of this information was aimed at frightening Americans. In retrospect, much of what I heard and "learned" in the months immediately following 9/11 was simply incorrect.

I became convinced that Muslims were my enemy. I am not talking about some sort of spiritual enmity in which the faiths are engaged in a competition to see who might convert more followers. I mean that I became convinced that all

10. I'm thinking here of the popular evangelical speaker who claimed to have been converted out of Islam and traveled to churches sharing his testimony, all while fabricating facts and speaking in "Arabic." Once some individuals who actually knew Arabic heard this man speak, he was exposed as a fraud.

Muslims wanted to kill me and my family, and that I needed to be very, very afraid.

In 2008, I traveled with Joy, my wife, to Northwood Church in Keller, Texas, for church-planter training. I don't know what I thought I would hear that day, but I did not hear that. Instead, I heard Bob Roberts talking about the way God had changed his life to love and live among the people I had long thought of as enemies. Bob spoke passionately about his love for the communist people of Vietnam. He grew excited talking about serving Afghans most of us would see only on the news. Bob was living a different way—a Jesus way—and I was enraptured.

He said something that stuck with me: "If you love your enemies, you eventually no longer have enemies." Several years later, I heard Jon Tyson, pastor of Church of the City New York, echo this sentiment. He said, "Those who love their enemies soon find they no longer have enemies—only neighbors." Perhaps Jon heard it from Bob. Or perhaps they both heard it from someone else. Or maybe when people are seeking to follow Jesus they arrive at the same conclusions. After the day-long training with Bob and his team, I got in the car and asked Joy, "What did you think?"

I'll never forget her reply: "That man is living the life you want to live."

She was right. Like she often is.

And from Bob I learned how to love those who had frightened me for years.

On June 12, 2016, a Muslim man entered a gay nightclub in Orlando, Florida, and murdered and wounded dozens of people. The next morning, a Monday, I passed a mosque as I was driving to our church's office. I had passed the mosque countless times, as it was on my route to the office, but today felt different. The Spirit prompted me: "You should go in there and tell them you love them. Show them the love of Jesus."

I hesitated for a moment and then whipped into the parking lot. Moments later I was talking to one of the mosque's leaders, attempting to explain why I wanted to meet the imam. I could tell he was skeptical. I left my contact information and continued on to the church. A few days later, I heard back. The imam agreed to meet me if he could bring another man. I told him I would do the same.

The next week we all met for tea. The imam and his friend sat down. After we exchanged pleasantries, I began to explain why I wanted to meet him. I don't remember exactly what I said, but I couldn't have been more than two minutes into my explanation when the imam interrupted me. "Can I ask you a question?"

"Sure," I said.

He was quick. "Do you think I'm going to hell?"

I squirmed for a moment and thought about how to answer. After a beat, I said, "That's what my tradition teaches, yes."

He smiled broadly. He even laughed. "Good," he said. "I think you're going to hell too. Now we can have an open conversation. Every so often we get Christian pastors who contact us and pretend to believe the same things that we believe. But we believe different things. That is why I'm a Muslim and you're a Christian. But you told me the truth. So I trust you."

And that's how some of our church leaders began a friendship with the leaders of a mosque just a few minutes down the road. Our church's elders hosted a dinner with the board from the mosque. They swapped stories about kids and spouses and sports. One of our members found out the imam enjoyed hunting, so he invited him to his ranch to deer hunt.

Early that morning the imam rose to pray and found two of our men reading the Bible and praying. He couldn't help but comment, "Who would have ever thought that I would be worshiping Allah and you would be worshiping Jesus and we would be friends?"

Over the years the imam and I have moved from colleagues to friends. You might be surprised to discover that the pressures of being clergy have a great deal of overlap, whether Christian or Muslim. When he was going through a particularly difficult situation, he sat in my office for over an hour while I listened to his struggles. I prayed with him and told him that I would do whatever I could to help him.

The two faith communities have become closer over the years. Imam leaders have invited us to iftar dinners as they break the fast during Ramadan, and we have invited them to our Easter Sunday. On one Easter, thirty or so Muslims joined us as we celebrated the resurrection of Jesus. After the service, our elders hosted a brunch to answer their questions about Easter. The first question made us chuckle: "We didn't hear anything about the Easter Bunny today. How does that fit in?"

Over the years we have participated in several theological dialogues and interviews. I have been invited to speak in two mosques in Houston. I have served with imams on a multifaith clergy council for law enforcement officers and their mental health. I have been invited to collaborate with Muslims in ways I never would have anticipated.

All of this happened because I chose to reach out in love to a group I once considered my enemy.

As you might imagine, not everyone was thrilled about us becoming friends with Muslims. Several people left our church. Some thought I was compromising on my theology.

One pastor told me that my befriending Muslims was simply giving them credibility. To be clear, my theology never changed. I still pray that each of my Muslim friends will encounter Jesus and choose to follow him.

My theology may not have changed, but living Jesus's theology did change me.

Jesus was always eating with people who made the overly religious nervous. They worried that Jesus was quietly condoning the behavior of sinners, but Jesus wanted to demonstrate the boundless love of the Father. It may be overly provocative to say so, but the love of God is, in the best sense of the word, promiscuous. It is indiscriminate; it is not selective. God lavishes love at the banquet table, and Jesus showed that so very well.

When our church campus was flooded in 2017, several pastor friends reached out to help us. But at the very front of that line was the mosque down the street. I don't know that they helped a single other church, but they helped us. Because you help your friends.

I may not have a fully formed theology of peacemaking. But I think the house of peacemaking is best built on the foundation of enemy love.

As Bono sings in the U2 song *Invisible*,

> There is no them
> There's only us.

5

Money Talks

Jesus on Possessions and the Poor

The Spirit of the Lord is on me, because he has anointed
me to preach good news to the poor.

—Luke 4:18

The function of freedom is to free someone else.
—Toni Morrison, commencement address
at Barnard College

My friend Joel (you'll hear more about him in chap. 8) regularly inspires me. Many years ago he became convinced that the Lord wanted him to live among the poor. So he did. He moved into the Fifth Ward of Houston, one of the most economically depressed sections of the city.

He began working at a church in the neighborhood, organizing a leadership development program for students. Late one evening Joel was walking to his car after a late night at his church. Two young men met him in the parking lot and pulled a gun on him. They demanded his car keys and his wallet. Joel pulled out his wallet and handed it to them. He was prepared to give them his keys when they turned and ran away.

Joel was shaken but unharmed.

A few days later, Joel and I met for lunch, and he told me this story. I was relieved to hear that he was unhurt. I asked if he was able to stop payment on his debit card before too much was taken.

"I was," he said.

And then he looked at me and said something I'll never forget.

"You know what they used it on, right?"

I thought about it for a second. They couldn't have purchased drugs with a debit card, could they? No, of course not. The transaction could be traced, and no self-respecting drug dealer would allow that. It had to be something they could purchase commercially and quickly.

"Liquor?" I may have added some other guesses. I don't remember. But I do remember what Joel said next.

"No, man. Taco Bell. Then they went to Wal-Mart and bought some diapers and formula."

That was the day my understanding of poverty fundamentally shifted.

In the West, poverty is moralized. Or, rather, the impoverished are regularly looked down on as immoral.

Like any large issue, poverty is more complex than we originally think. We tend to vilify the poor in the West partly because of our economic system. The American dream, after all, is that with enough hard work and determination, anyone can make it and have it better than their parents. It's hard not to believe this myth when you read, for example, the story of Frederick Douglass. Douglass was a slave who learned how to read, escaped from slavery, and eventually became a preacher and well-known public figure in the United States.[1]

We hear story after story of people like Douglass in American lore—and for good reason. For all our nation's flaws, this sort of thing truly is possible in the land of the free. Many people are able to rise above their station through hard work and determination. I continue to believe that many of life's obstacles can indeed be overcome, and we should celebrate those who work with grit and determination toward that end.

The problem with this way of thinking is that we tend to apply the converse, even when it is not true. In other words, if hard work and determination can help someone rise above their station, what are we to believe about someone who doesn't rise above their station? At best, we think them content. We imagine that they like their lives, their families, their jobs, or their neighborhoods. And because they are happy, they have chosen a particular outcome. That's our best assumption.

But we regularly don't think the best of them. We often think they are lazy. If someone is poor, we reason, it is because they are not willing to work. If someone is without the things they need, then many of us think they deserve to live in poverty. Being poor is an outcome of a choice, pure and simple. Or so the reasoning goes.

We don't tend to think of how poverty concentrated in a single neighborhood, city, or region can compound into disastrous effects. In the city of Houston, the compounded effects

1. Frederick Douglass, *Narrative of the Life of Frederick Douglass: An American Slave*, independently published, 2019.

of poverty can be seen simply by looking at demographic maps. Generally speaking, the poorest parts of Houston are those on the east side of the city. Those same parts of the city are without new church plants, without grocery stores (and fresh produce), with greater health concerns, without doctors, with failing or struggling schools, and with higher crime rates. All of these issues are intertwined. And almost all of them are because of poverty.[2]

If people don't have enough money, they can't donate enough to sustain a church. If people don't have enough money, they can't shop at a large supermarket. Likewise, they can't afford fresh produce so must live on processed foods. Over time, a diet made up of primarily processed foods leads to health issues. Most doctors' offices are in a nicer part of town where they might have more earning power and where crime will be less of a concern. Because the adults don't make much money, they can't raise more money for their neighborhood school, can't donate extra school supplies, and often aren't at home to help with homework. Instead, they're working a second job to try to make ends meet. Without robust parent involvement, discipline issues at school skyrocket, absences mount, and homework goes undone. As a result, the schools struggle or fail.

And what happens to young men who can't get enough to eat or enough education to find a decent job?

If they do not have guidance, they end up robbing my friend Joel in the church parking lot. And if they are arrested, they add to the destructive cycle in their community.

The more this cycle perpetuates, the harder it is for the community to recover, and the issues compound. People stop

2. These issues cannot be cleanly separated from race and ethnicity. To be sure, much of the poverty in Houston is a result of generations of discrimination, segregation, redlining, and the like.

thinking of rejuvenating the neighborhood. They start thinking about how to escape the neighborhood.

Each of these problems traces back to poverty.

Let's take crime, for example. I used to think of crime as something that evil people do. And, yes, there are vile people who perpetrate all sorts of heinous crimes. Also, crime as such is no respecter of wealth, as there are plenty of wealthy people who commit crimes. In Houston we still remember Enron. (For those who don't remember: Enron was a Houston-based energy company driven into bankruptcy through intricate accounting fraud and corruption at the highest levels. Enron was a Fortune 500 company with billions in revenue but without a moral compass; those at the top ruined the lives of thousands of employees by defrauding them of their pensions and retirement funds. Clearly not all crime is tied to poverty.)

But a great deal of crime begins with poverty. Those who are hungry have often resorted to stealing bread. Survival is a powerful instinct, and if people do not see a way forward, they will break the law in order to provide for themselves or their family. This, of course, does not justify criminal activity. It does, however, help us understand how community economics contribute to overall crime activity within that same community. The correlation is difficult to quantify, but it stands to reason that many crime-riddled neighborhoods could become safer if their economic status could rise as well. Community organizations and revitalization efforts are usually directed specifically at economic development for this very reason.[3]

3. I'm reminded here of Malcolm Gladwell's examination of the criminology theory called "the broken window theory," in which small bits of disrepair and disarray build on one another, leading to more crime. Conversely, if those

Could hard work and determination make a difference in these neighborhoods? Of course. Is it enough? Not likely. People do make it out of difficult circumstances. But those people are the minority. It is fairly common knowledge that the zip code where you are born is a fairly accurate predictor of your future outcomes—from education to income. In other words, if you are born in an impoverished zip code, you are more likely to have less education, less income, and more health issues, and you are more likely to be involved in crime in some way. For people who want a better life, their options are limited: accept a life with built-in disadvantages, find a way to escape, or turn to crime. James Baldwin put it succinctly: "Anyone who has ever struggled with poverty knows how extremely expensive it is to be poor."[4]

Poverty can be overcome, but it often works against people from the beginning. And if poverty is such an indicator of future success, if it hamstrings people from becoming the best version of themselves—from being healthy, from being educated, from having a healthy family—then it stands to reason that someone ought to care about addressing it. After all, the kingdom vision is one of flourishing, of life. Those in the kingdom do not have the luxury of not caring about those in need, for they are too busy answering the question, "And who is my neighbor?" Once those in the kingdom realize they are surrounded by neighbors, they want to see the vision of the kingdom take hold in everyone's life, for everyone to experience the life God intends for each of us.

---

things are taken care of, crime is theoretically much lower. For more on this theory, see Malcolm Gladwell, *The Tipping Point: How Little Things Can Make a Big Difference* (New York: Little, Brown, 2000), 133–35.

4. James Baldwin, *Nobody Knows My Name: More Notes of a Native Son* (New York: Vintage, 1993), 62.

The God of the Bible cares deeply for the poor. The Bible talks about the poor more than anyone else—other than God himself. There are more than two thousand verses in the Bible that talk about the poor, justice, and poverty. If the verses are limited to mentioning only the poor and generosity, the number is still approximately three hundred verses. As anyone who has traveled in the Majority World can testify, poverty is a massive global obstacle.[5]

In the Old Testament, God casts a vision for the nation of Israel that they would be a people reflecting his character. Part of that vision is a community that looks after the families and individuals among them who have less than what they need.

Let's begin with the laws for landowners involving the harvesting of grain. Leviticus 19:9–10 issues a very plain edict: "When you reap the harvest of your land, you are not to reap to the very edge of your field or gather the gleanings of your harvest. Do not strip your vineyard bare or gather its fallen grapes. Leave them for the poor and the resident alien; I am the LORD your God."

Those who had land would harvest grain for storage and sales. It was their livelihood. But, according to Scripture, those who had grain were intended to share it with those who did not. They did this by not harvesting all the way to the

5. I first heard the two-thousand verses number from the organization Sojourners and the three-hundred verses number from the relief organization Compassion International. At the time of writing, both organizations have the respective numbers on their websites. I've heard similar figures from Rich Stearns, formerly of World Vision, and World Relief. Some of these verses are not prescriptive on how to treat the poor, but they buttress the idea that economic security is primary in the mind of God. However one chooses to examine the Scriptures, God's heart for the poor is apparent.

edges of their fields. Similarly, the Lord commanded grapes to be left behind for those in need.

We see this law regarding the gleaning of grain play out in the book of Ruth. This is significant in that the law was not merely a theoretical suggestion; it was put into practice. In Ruth 2:3, Ruth goes to the field of Boaz to gather grain behind the harvesters, meaning that the harvesters were explicitly instructed to leave grain behind for those in the community who did not have enough to eat. Naomi and Ruth—both widows—would have been in a precarious economic situation. But with people like Boaz in the community, they had enough food to eat.

The command among the Israelites, however, was broader than providing food. In Leviticus 25:35–36 they are commanded, "If your brother becomes destitute and cannot sustain himself among you, you are to support him as an alien or temporary resident, so that he can continue to live among you. Do not profit or take interest from him, but fear your God and let your brother live among you."

If a family is unable to feed themselves, those with grain are to make certain the family can gather grain and grapes. Furthermore, if a family loses everything, then the community is to take up the responsibility to care for them, "as an alien or temporary resident." In the Middle East, a foreigner is treated with great respect—as a highly honored guest. The best food is presented for a guest, even if it is the last bit of food in the house. For those of us in the West, such hospitality may not make sense, but those hearing this command understood perfectly. If anyone was unable to provide for themselves, those individuals were treated well, like honored guests. Within the community of God, we are called to share what we have, even if we do not have much.

Many years ago I went into the home of a poor Palestinian family in the West Bank. We were greeted by a woman and her children. I do not remember if the woman was married; if she was, her husband must have been at work. There were probably ten of us in our group. She had very little money; her accommodations made that obvious. Yet she insisted on honoring us by making tea and serving cookies and hard candies, all on the nicest dishes she had to offer. Meanwhile, she drank no tea and had no cookies. I wondered if we took the last of what she had. I do not know, but I do know she was immensely honored to treat us as guests.

Her generous hospitality reminds me of the command placed before the people of Israel, except in reverse: treat those among you who are poor as honored guests. Sojourners and strangers are not to be shamed or robbed of their dignity. They are to be treated as those who have been created in the image of God and are deserving of having their basic needs met.

These sorts of commands are throughout the Old Testament. By way of example:

> If there is a poor person among you, one of your brothers within any of your city gates in the land the Lord your God is giving you, do not be hardhearted or tightfisted toward your poor brother. Instead, you are to open your hand to him and freely loan him enough for whatever need he has. (Deut. 15:7–8)

> Give to him, and don't have a stingy heart when you give, and because of this the Lord your God will bless you in all your work and in everything you do. (Deut. 15:10)

> Provide justice for the needy and the fatherless;
> uphold the rights of the oppressed and the destitute.
> (Ps. 82:3)

The one who oppresses the poor insults their Maker,
but one who is kind to the needy honors Him. (Prov.
14:31)

God cares so much for the poor that he commanded his people to hold a Jubilee feast every fifty years. At this time debts were cancelled, lands were returned to clans, and slaves were to be freed.[6]

Verse after verse reminds Israel to care for those who are poor. In doing so, they honor God. Which is why, I think, Jesus and his earliest followers cared a great deal about taking care of the poor as well.

In Luke 6:20–21 Jesus says,

Blessed are you who are poor,
because the kingdom of God is yours.
Blessed are you who are hungry now,
because you will be filled.

When a rich man asked Jesus what he needed to do to have eternal life, the Lord commanded him to sell everything he owned and then follow him (Matt. 19:16–21).

When Zacchaeus came to faith in Jesus, the way he proved that his salvation was genuine was to give half of his possessions to the poor and to give back four times over to those he might have cheated (Luke 19:1–10).

When Jesus saw a widow give generously, he commended her saying, "This poor widow has put in more than all of them [the rich]" (Luke 21:3).

6. This year is described in Lev. 25. My understanding is that there is no record, however, that the people of Israel ever celebrated the Jubilee. I suppose it may have felt too radical even to them.

Over and over, Jesus indicated that our relationship to our resources was an indicator of our relationship to God.

Early in his ministry, Jesus entered a synagogue, opened up a scroll of the prophet Isaiah, and chose to read the following section:

> The Spirit of the Lord is on me,
> because he has anointed me
> to preach good news to the poor.
> He has sent me
> to proclaim release to the captives
> and recovery of sight to the blind,
> to set free the oppressed,
> to proclaim the year of the Lord's favor. (Luke
> 4:18–19)[7]

After he did this, the Bible says he sat down and then said, "Today as you listen, this Scripture has been fulfilled" (Luke 4:21).

Why did Jesus choose this passage from Isaiah? And why did he say that it was fulfilled in his presence?

There was a time when I understood Jesus to mean that the gospel of salvation was good news to the poor simply because it was available to anyone, including the poor. That is, of course, true. But Jesus declared his presence to be good news to the poor for a very different reason. Jesus is the kingdom and the way of God embodied. Those who choose to follow Jesus will be grateful for having received grace. And in receiving that grace, they will want to live as God would have them live. And how would God have them live? God would have them be generous and share from their abundance with

7. Jesus is quoting from Isa. 61:1–2.

89

those who do not have enough. In the grace of God through Jesus the festival of Jubilee might finally come to pass, and those who are overcome by financial pressures will be given aid by those who can come to their rescue.

Jesus preaches good news to the poor because when people believe in Jesus, they share what they have with the poor. The gospel of the kingdom creates a generous people. In light of the generosity of God toward us—bringing us from death to life—we now look to extend that life to others. Just like tree roots share nutrients, just like the forest perpetually works to create life, those in the kingdom recognize their part in sustaining the lives of their neighbors. Cooperation and collaboration are kingdom traits indeed.

Some have noted that Jesus connected his arrival to the concept of Jubilee: not only would he have us be saved spiritually, but he would introduce a radical way of relating to one another in which money would not be supreme.[8] In a day when most prisoners were held because of debts and when the poor were often oppressed, wouldn't it be good news for a new community to come into being where the poor could experience freedom?

I think this is why the earliest believers shared their possessions, as recorded in Acts 2 and Acts 4. In Acts 2:45 we read, "They sold their possessions and property and distributed the proceeds to all, as any had need." Similarly, Acts 4:32

8. See, e.g., Walter Brueggemann, *Theology of the Old Testament: Testimony, Dispute, Advocacy* (Minneapolis: Fortress, 2012). Brueggemann addresses the concept of Jubilee on page 189, but I believe he counts himself among scholars who remain unsure if Israel ever actually celebrated Jubilee, as mentioned in note 6. Verses like Isa. 61:1, which Jesus quotes in Luke 4:18–19, are a sort of Jubilee reference (Brueggemann, 208) finding completion in Jesus's kingdom, where those who have material excess share with those who do not—as in, e.g., Acts 2 and Acts 4.

says that among the earliest believers, "no one claimed that any of his possessions was his own, but instead they held everything in common." Generosity was held in high esteem. In fact, when a couple attempted to feign generosity rather than being truly generous, they died on the spot, stricken by God (Acts 5:1–11).

A golden thread of generosity runs through the Bible, pointing over and over to God's concern for the poor and the desire that his people share that concern. From Israel to Jesus to the church, the poor matter to God in the Bible. They matter to God a great deal. They matter so much that they are mentioned more than just about anything or anyone else in the Bible.

They matter so much that when God became flesh, he ushered in his kingdom not from a palace but from a stable. They matter so much that God first announced the kingdom to shepherds, not to celebrities. Jesus chose to identify with the poor most of his human life, apparently having few possessions despite being a craftsman.[9]

The poor matter to God.

Therefore, the poor ought to matter to us.

⁓

Caring about the poor is sometimes politicized. I once preached a sermon in which I mentioned some of the verses highlighted in this chapter, pointing out the fact that our church ought to care for the poor. Afterward I heard that

---

9. The Greek word used to describe the profession of Jesus's father, Joseph, is *tektōn*. Although we usually translate the word as "carpenter," he was more likely trained primarily as a stonemason. If you visit Galilee, you will see that there are very few trees and an abundance of stone. He may have been trained to work with both stone and wood. Whatever the case, he did not support himself primarily as a *tektōn* but as an itinerant rabbi.

some were surprised I was "a liberal." I can understand their confusion. But if there is any area where I feel confident that Jesus would be classified as "liberal," it would be his concern for the poor.

This is not to say that God doesn't value work. Work was part of human life before sin. God created work to be good. In the New Testament, Paul tells us that we ought to aim to live a quiet life and to work with our hands (1 Thess. 4:11). He also tells us that if we do not provide for our family, then we are worse than an unbeliever (1 Tim. 5:8). It is good and right to work hard, to provide for those in our circle.

At the same time, the Bible is clear about our responsibility to care for those who are impoverished.

After all, the word "liberal" means "generous."

As usual, the devil is in the details. Sometimes when I talk about this topic, people mistakenly think I am advocating for specific government policies. That is not my goal in this chapter, although I will say that I am often in favor of us leveraging resources to help those in need. My point is that if God cares for the poor, then the church must care for the poor, and we must organize our finances as such—both individually and communally. If the church should be known by its difference, how beautiful would it be for a church to be intentionally generous in the midst of a materialistic society? As we are liberal in our generosity, we model the liberal generosity shown by God through Jesus.

The great obstacle we face in regard to generosity is that of fear. In many cases greed is rooted in fear—usually the fear of losing financial security. Occasionally, greed is rooted in a different sort of fear, the fear of not being respected. We often convince ourselves that if we have more money, we will gain the admiration of those around us. There is certainly plenty of evidence to support such a conclusion, although just how genuine that admiration is would likely be a matter of debate. Others are driven by yet another sort of fear, the fear of not having a certain set of experiences or standard of living that will, they believe, bring happiness. This is a reason why those who have come to faith in Jesus are to be marked with generosity: we have experienced a depth of love that casts out fear. We know that all we possess has been given to us by the gracious hand of God, and we trust that every single breath we draw is a gift from him. First John 4:18 says, "perfect love drives out fear." The perfect love of God in Christ moves his people to a stunning generosity for which we ought to be known.

The namesake of my city, Sam Houston, is reported to have made a large donation to Independence Baptist Church after being baptized, paying half of Pastor Rufus Burleson's salary. When asked why he did so, Houston is reported to have said, "Well, preacher, you've baptized my pocketbook!" Houston went on to become one of the most generous philanthropists in Texas, funding many charitable works designed to help those most in need.[10]

Houston is an excellent example of how faith might transform the generosity of an individual. But as influential as a single individual can be, the power of the church has always been greater. The church's strength has been in its collective generosity, in its desire to distribute to any as he or she has need (Acts 2:45). The kingdom is marked by a new economy, one where generosity is the primary marker of success.

10. Sam Houston's conversion and baptism is part of Texas history lore, and the accounts and precise quotes vary from source to source. Whatever Houston said, he clearly said something to the effect of his pocketbook being baptized, and he became immensely generous after his conversion.

What might it mean for those of us who have "baptized pocketbooks" to put them to use for Jesus and his kingdom? How might a local congregation live among the community in such a way that their relationships make it almost impossible for anyone to live in financial need? It's a lofty ideal, to be sure, but it's also a mark of the kingdom. When the church decides to live in generosity of relationship as well as finance, then the church can truly understand the needs of the community and serve in ways that are truly helpful.

How might the church live with relational and financial generosity? The answer can be summarized in two words: creativity and relationship.

When I speak of creativity with regard to caring for the poor, I mean that there is no universal solution prescribed in the Bible for precisely how this goal ought to be achieved. There is the model of intentional generosity in Leviticus and Deuteronomy. There is also the communal life of shared resources in Acts 2 and 4. Later in the New Testament there is a moment where a special offering is taken up by one church to help those in need in another church (2 Cor. 8:7–15).

I think if there was a specific way we were to go about caring for the poor, it would be more clearly prescribed in the New Testament or the writings of the earliest Christians. In both of those places we simply find believers creatively sharing their resources where there is need—a model we ought to aspire to emulate. Since there is no obvious methodology for generosity given in Scripture, there are numerous ways we might go about this. Whatever we do, however, the church must find a way to help those in need, no matter the cultural context, because we are people marked by the generosity of God.

I've been stunned by the creativity with which believers approach the command to love and serve the poor. At our church we've taken some fairly straightforward steps. We have a fund set aside to help anyone in the community who is in financial need, and a team oversees the distribution of those funds.[11] We also have a community garden that distributes the produce to those in need, specifically delivering it to a food bank located in a food desert.[12] We offer free English classes to immigrants in our city. We connect refugees and immigrants who need assistance navigating the legal and federal labyrinth with those who can help them. None of these are unique to our church; many other churches do similar things.

Other communities have undertaken more creative and expansive efforts. Shane Claiborne, founder of the Simple Way community in Philadelphia, has worked to create an organization called Simple Homes. Simple Homes purchases abandoned homes in the city and then works together with those needing a home to repair the house and get it up to city code. Then Simple Homes gifts the home to the family. Dignity is maintained, and homelessness is reduced.[13]

Claiborne drew inspiration from people like Dorothy Day, who helped create the Catholic Worker Movement in the 1930s, seeking to create better conditions for the American working class. One summer, Joy and I visited our niece in Portland, Oregon. One night as we were walking through her

---

11. I have heard some argue that the early church helped only the poor who were believers. I disagree with this statement for two reasons. First, in Gal. 2:10 Paul says, "They asked only that we would remember the poor, which I had made every effort to do." This sounds like a universal helping of the poor, not only for believers. Second, the commands in Leviticus and Deuteronomy were to help the poor of the entire community, not just the Israelites. It makes sense that the sentiment of broad generosity would permeate the early churches as well.

12. The USDA defines a food desert as an area with limited access to healthy and affordable food. For more information, go to www.usda.gov.

13. See www.simplehomes.org.

neighborhood, we saw a refrigerator and table in a front yard. As we walked closer to inspect, we found a sign: "Take whatever you need. Donate whatever you can share." We looked inside the refrigerator to find a good selection of foods. There were dry goods in a box next to the refrigerator, and you were welcome to sit at the table to eat. Next to the table were a few copies of the *Catholic Worker* newspaper.[14] As best we could tell, this was the effort of a single family being creative to help those in their community.

Other church-related organizations have taken seriously the call to help those in need. The Cornerstone Assistance Network in Fort Worth has a case-manager model in which they help individuals move from need (sometimes as severe as chronic homelessness) to full employment and independent living. They do this by incentivizing each step that an individual takes in the process. If you fill out a certain number of job applications or take a certain number of training hours in a given week, then you receive assistance for the next week. As clients and case managers work through the process, clients take steps toward financial wholeness.[15]

One group I've long admired is the Bruderhof. The Bruderhof is an Anabaptist-ish community founded by Eberhard Arnold in Sinntal, Germany, in 1920.[16] Arnold envisioned a community living by the teachings of Jesus that eschewed

14. The *Catholic Worker* newspaper was founded by Dorothy Day and Peter Maurin in 1933 to highlight the plight of the working class.

15. Cornerstone has been lauded by many, including Princeton University, as one of the best models of poverty reduction in the nation.

16. Dietrich Bonhoeffer modeled much of his underground seminary at Finkenwalde and Zingst after the Bruderhof, going so far as to call his seminary the Bruderhaus. *Bruderhof* means "place of brothers" while *Bruderhaus* means "house of brothers." Bonhoeffer met with Eberhard Arnold's son, Hardy, in London in 1934 and used much of what he learned about the Bruderhof in the formation of the seminary.

private property and instead shared resources, taking their inspiration from the model of shared resources in Acts 2 and Acts 4.[17] Community members do a number of jobs to support one another.[18] Anyone willing to take on the rule of the community can join it, meaning that those who are impoverished can be part of the community and have their needs met.

We often forget that Martin Luther King Jr. and many of those who marched for civil rights also worked diligently to help the poor. King is best remembered for his "I Have a Dream" speech on the National Mall, but he was in Washington, DC, as part of the March on Washington for Jobs and Freedom. The Southern Christian Leadership Conference believed that civil rights for Black families must be paired with economic opportunity. In my mind, thousands of citizens marching in Washington, DC, certainly qualifies as a creative solution to help those in need.

One of the most creative families I know on this front is my cousin Gene and his wife, Nancy. They are always opening their home, sharing a meal, handing out rolls of quarters at the local laundromat, and allowing people to live in their basement. They may not have created an organization (yet I wouldn't put anything past them), but they are certainly creative in the ways they seek to help their neighbors. That's the beautiful thing about generosity; it doesn't depend on your larger church for you to get involved. If you recognize the generosity of God in your life, then you can begin demonstrating generosity with whatever you have.

17. You can read more about the Bruderhof in Clare Stober, *Another Life Is Possible: Insights from 100 Years Together* (Rifton, NY: Plough, 2020).

18. I've long been a fan of the Bruderhof's theological journal and resources, curated under an organization called Plough. You can read more at www.plough.com.

Once you, your church, or your organization gets creative in its mindset to help those in need, you simply need generosity. The more generous people are, the more that can be done. Food, shelter, job training, and the like all require funding. I've consistently been amazed at the way Christians respond in generosity when they see a creative solution to poverty. In 2017, when Houston was flooded by Hurricane Harvey, I saw donations from churches across the country come pouring in to our church's campus. One of the largest Christian relief organizations in the world, World Vision, set up a distribution hub in our parking lot for a time. People from all over the world made donations to help people they did not know who had suddenly become homeless.

Likewise, over the years I've pastored, I've asked our congregation to give sacrificially to help Afghan refugees, Ukrainian refugees, those struggling with medical debt in our community, flood victims, tornado victims, earthquake victims, wildfire victims, the underground church, and all sorts of other causes. Each time I've made a request to help those in need—as long as there was a workable creative solution in place—our church responded with great generosity. I once heard someone say that giving follows vision. I think he meant that people will give to a project that has a defined picture of a preferred future. In one sense, I agree, but I tend to think that generosity follows creativity, particularly when it comes to serving the poor. We have not always had a long-term vision for how to heal the systemic issues at the root of a problem, but when we have worked to bring a creative solution to help the impoverished in our community, our city, and beyond, I have seen people give generously time and time again.

Israel was commanded to share their grain and their grapes with their poor neighbors. With grain and grapes, even the poorest in the community could grind wheat for bread and squeeze juice for wine. I can't help but notice that these are the same elements present on the table when we gather for Communion. The very items God's people are commanded to share in Levitical law are the same items used to commemorate his great generosity of sacrificial death. As Jesus broke bread and said "This is my body," he sat in a borrowed upper room. I cannot help but wonder if he also shared bread and wine provided by a generous benefactor. As best we can tell, he owned nothing, and the hospitality of the region was rich, so I suspect this was the case. Just as grain and grapes were left for the poor in Leviticus, Jesus may have benefited from the grain and grapes of another.

This strikes me as exactly something Jesus would do. Each time we partake of the bread or the cup, we are keenly aware that Jesus was generous to each of us, but perhaps we should also consider that this commemorative meal was made possible by the generosity of an unnamed other, creating a spiral of giving intended to expand outward into the life of the church.

The cross of Christ is the most generous response possible by God to the deep need of humanity—the need for redemption. As I mentioned earlier, our default position is to operate from fear, and fear often results in greed. We hoard that which we believe we will lose. And in our fearful hoarding, we betray ourselves and one another, leaving ourselves in need of redemption. When we were in need of redemption, God gave of himself and became flesh, he moved into the neighborhood,[19] and then freely gave of his love. He did so by sharing a meal and

19. The Message translation of John 1:14 says, "The Word became flesh and blood, and moved into the neighborhood."

then by allowing himself to be hung on a cross. It is a solution simultaneously individual, cosmic, and radically self-giving.

I believe there is something within us that knows the cross is true, because the cross is an example of someone helping another without good reason. No good reason, that is, unless you believe that God has in fact created humans in his image and does in fact deeply love them. People have responded in faith to the cross because it is the most creative and the most generous of all solutions, and I believe that they want to model that same sort of creativity and generosity when they see a need they might be able to address. It is acting on behalf of those who cannot act on behalf of themselves. Bonhoeffer called this sort of work *Stellvertretung*, which can be translated as "vicarious representative action."[20] He understood the cross as the ultimate representation of this vicarious representative action. Humanity was condemned by sin and could do nothing to rescue itself. Only Jesus could intercede. His intercession is our example. Just as Jesus did what only he could do in order to help us, we are now called to vicarious representative action for our neighbors.

Jesus called such action love. What might we do to model the generous love of Jesus by demonstrating generosity toward our neighbors? If we are to love our neighbor, let us do so with the creativity and the generosity of the cross, modeling our lives after our Savior.

20. Bonhoeffer uses this phrase in a number of his works but most fully develops the concept in his *Ethics*. See Dietrich Bonhoeffer, *Ethics*, vol. 6 in Dietrich Bonhoeffer Works, ed. Clifford J. Green, trans. Reinhard Krauss, Charles C. West, and Douglas W. Stott (Minneapolis: Fortress, 2005), 231–38, 275, 282. I more fully unpack this theological concept in my doctoral dissertation. See Steven Bezner, "Understanding the World Better Than It Understands Itself: The Theological Hermeneutics of Dietrich Bonhoffer" (PhD diss., Baylor University, 2008), 140–94, https://baylor-ir.tdl.org/server/api/core/bit streams/4a2559f3-6d66-45de-8515-095eed28986e/content.

6

With Pleasure

Jesus on Sexuality

You are not your own, for you were bought at a price.
So glorify God with your body.

—1 Corinthians 6:20

Mortification is training in love.
—Zena Hitz, *A Philosopher Looks
at the Religious Life*

I debated a great deal about whether to include a chapter on sex in this book. In the end, I decided to do so because it is something my church members ask me about regularly. I can only assume other Christians are curious as well—so curious, in fact, I would not be surprised to find that on perusing the table of contents some have turned to this chapter first. I hesitated to include this chapter because, well, is there a more uncomfortable combination for public conversation than Christians and sex? Talking about

Christianity and sex is the opposite of a perfect pairing, such as, say, peanut butter and chocolate. If Reese's Peanut Butter Cups are the perfect candy that brings a smile to everyone's face (and they are, in my humble opinion), the combination of Christianity and sex is its painful antonym, leading to pursed lips and a collective loss of appetite. I suspect that just as some will turn first to this chapter, others might skip it altogether.

This is, in part, because evangelical Christians, particularly those in my denominational heritage, have long struggled to find substantive theological ways to talk about sex. I'm reminded of the old quip that used to float around churches: "Sex is dirty and awful and sinful, and you ought to save it for the one you love." As one who came of age in the 1980s and 1990s, I can say that our vocabulary may have changed some, but we have rarely been accused of pastoral precision in our discussions about sex and sexuality.

Our struggles have painted us into any number of corners. On the one hand, we overvalued sex, specifically virginity. Whatever good may have come out of the "True Love Waits" campaign within evangelicalism in the 1990s and 2000s—and there was certainly some good—there was also a great deal of shame. Anyone in evangelical youth circles in those days who became sexually active prior to marriage could not help but feel as if they had given away the greatest gift they could give. And, if we are being specific, the pressure was (and may still be) primarily on girls being held responsible for the actions of boys. After all, boys sow wild oats, but girls garner a reputation for being loose. As we attempted to raise the value of sex, we somehow made it less valuable. If virginity is the prize to be protected, what is left to protect once virginity is gone?

On a theological note, some of us must grapple with the fact that for years we gathered students for Bible studies and lifted sexual morality to a place that seemed equal with belief in God. In caring so much about sex, we unintentionally devalued the divine. We accidentally made sexual morality the goal of the Christian life, not the outcome of an encounter with Jesus. Granted, subtlety is not easy with adolescents. But I must confess my own complicity in this way of ministry; until I awoke to the gospel of the kingdom, I was teaching something other than the beauty of the way of Jesus.

After the push for purity, some Christian leaders swung the pendulum too far in the other direction (as we tend to do), speaking of sex in ways that were little different from other groups. We stopped speaking of sex as something that is sacramental—the place where the divine and the earthly meet. We escaped the evangelical anxiety regarding the dirtiness of sex but exchanged it for pragmatism, speaking in ways that abandoned any hint of the spiritual or the ethical. As a result, sex became a sort of sermonic gimmick, used to bolster church attendance rather than as an invitation into a foretaste of the ecstatic union with Christ.

To make matters more complicated, our culture—and some other Christian traditions—have little interest in our theology of sex, having moved on some time ago. My denomination and broader theological stream holds to the traditional Christian sexual ethic—that sexual activity is reserved for marriage—but I also know that shifting attitudes surrounding sexuality and faith often make such an admission a nonstarter for conversation. Rather than focusing solely on the ethics of sexual activity of individuals, I want to talk about a few other aspects of sexuality that drive the kingdom vision, particularly self-denial (also known as mortification) and hospitality. Each of these, I believe, plays into our themes of expanding life in the same counterintuitive kingdom ways. I do not want to minimize personal sexual ethics; I want to give a more robust vision of what a church seeking to live out sexual purity might look like.[1] Jesus and Paul both assumed (and even argued) that many people faithful to the kingdom vision would choose to forgo sex in order to focus more fully on service to God. But that assumption seems to have been forgotten by many congregations, leaving those who want to choose a life of faithful chastity out in the relational cold. If Christians are to take Jesus seriously, then celibacy and self-denial must be valid options, specifically in the presence of a supportive congregation ready to welcome the sexually celibate into deep community akin to that of family.

Part of this task will require us to reenvision sex itself. Is it possible to have a conversation about sexuality that does not overvalue sex or strip it of its sacramental nature? Can we speak of sex as something that is beautiful, complex, good, but not ultimate? Can we envision a community that provides a fulfilling way of life for those who decide to live without sex?

Obviously, I think the answer is yes. To do so, we must approach sexuality a bit differently than do many other popular treatments.

The main difference: I am not arguing for a universal approach to human sexuality. I am, instead, arguing for a specifically Christian sexual ethic for those who are part of the

1. Any number of scholars have written about the Christian vision of sexuality in a more comprehensive way than I could ever hope to achieve in one chapter. See, for example, the work of Preston Sprinkle, Jackie Hill Perry, Sam Allberry, Rachel Gilson, Christopher Yuan, and Rosaria Butterfield, among others.

Christian community, and I am hoping to envision what a community living this ethic might look like for those who have embraced the call to celibacy. Those outside the Christian faith will likely find this particular approach to sex unappealing. My goal is not to convince those outside the faith that they ought to view sex and sexuality through a Christian lens. It is, instead, to convince Christians that having a distinct view of sex and sexuality is good and, if viewed properly, strengthens our view of the church. I hope to show that sex is not ultimate and that humans can have a satisfying life apart from sex—in part because of the power of Christian community.

I don't speak about sex and sexuality lightly. I serve as a pastor and have served in some form of pastoral ministry for almost thirty years. Some of the most agonizing pastoral conversations over those years have been with people who desperately want to honor Jesus with their lives and yet find themselves wanting things that are outside the traditional Christian sexual vision. I won't overtly detail any of those pastoral conversations here, but as someone who has had his own struggles with lust of the flesh over the years, I can openly admit my empathy for those who struggle in ways I do not—because I too often have desires I wish I did not have.

I write this chapter with several groups of people in mind. To begin, I am thinking of the single adults in my congregation. Some of them are young and have never been married. Others of them are divorced. Others still have been widowed. They earnestly strive to live a life of fidelity to the sexual vision portrayed in the New Testament when every message outside of the church tells them that such a quest is foolhardy. I also think of those in my congregation whose sexual desires are not heterosexual: the married father who believes he is gay, the single woman who tells me she is a lesbian, the woman who confesses to me she is asexual, and many others. They often find themselves torn between believing what their church teaches regarding sex and what their church teaches regarding authenticity. They fear that authentic confession on this topic, which they have been taught should bring deeper understanding and acceptance, would instead lead to outright rejection.[2] Furthermore, I think of those who have discovered sex within marriage to be something other than fulfilling and now grapple with what that means for their future. I have faith that the way of Jesus would not leave us without a path to experience deep satisfaction, so I will argue that the church community is one of the ways we might experience the very satisfaction for which we hunger.

Most people, I believe, are not simply looking for sex but are instead searching for intimacy. My hypothesis is that the church can be a place to find such intimacy—but it must be intentionally pursued. Sex is often referred to as intimacy, but the two are not synonymous. Intimacy is the ability to be emotionally transparent and vulnerable with another individual, to share thoughts, feelings, desires, and dreams, to feel no need to "playact" in front of the other. Ideally, sex is the physical outworking of emotional intimacy. As two people come to deep familiarity and comfort with each other, they are able to engage in the physically vulnerable activity of sex. Granted, some sex is simply driven by lusty physical attraction—often referred to as "hooking up." But while humans can live without hooking up, they cannot flourish

2. The ability to confess these desires (whether acted upon or not) is often a matter of life and death, where fear of rejection leads to increased rates of suicide.

without intimacy. Sex is not necessary for individual flourishing; emotional intimacy is. For those who choose to forgo sex out of faithfulness to God, friendships within the church should (must?) be a place where intimacy can be found.

As I look at the Bible and evidence from the earliest days of the church, I am convinced that Christians have—from the very beginning—had a peculiar sexual ethic that emphasized self-denial and treating one another as family, particularly those who were unmarried. In doing so, everyone was afforded true intimacy, even if they denied themselves the physical pleasure of sex. One thing about us Baptists, for all our flaws (and there are many we could discuss), is that we strive to take the Bible seriously. So, while I may stand before Jesus one day and find I was gravely mistaken on this topic, I must confess that this is my best understanding of what Jesus and the New Testament authors were teaching.[3]

Some of my friends and family will no doubt disagree with what I write in this chapter, but I hope they will at least agree that this treatment is a good-faith engagement with the Scriptures, that it was handled with pastoral love and grace, and that it reflected Jesus in its approach.

When we talk about sex, we must talk about desire. As philosopher James K. A. Smith points out, we are what we love.[4] In *Desiring the Kingdom*, Smith argues against a view of

---

3. I acknowledge that there is a burgeoning group of people within Christianity who argue for a different view of sexuality and faith. They claim that sexuality needs no boundary other than adult consent. I have read their scholarship, argumentation, and reasoning. In the end, I find their reading of the New Testament unconvincing.

4. See James K. A. Smith, *You Are What You Love: The Spiritual Power of Habit* (Grand Rapids: Brazos, 2016).

humanity driven by our minds and instead rather effectively argues that we act on the basis of what we want. Once we know what we want, we will begin to better understand our actions. We are driven by our gut—the deepest yearnings within us—and those gut-level yearnings drive us to act.[5]

Those deep desires form us, causing us to search for satiation and pushing us into action. Some of these activities become regular and familiar—liturgies of sorts, in which we find meaning and purpose. Our culture is hypersexualized; few would debate such a claim. C. S. Lewis noted our trend toward unhealthy sexual appetites in his classic book *Mere Christianity*: "You can get a large audience together for a striptease act—that is, to watch a girl undress on the stage. Now suppose you came to a country where you could fill a theatre by simply bringing a covered plate on to the stage and then slowly lifting the cover so as to let every one see, just before the lights went out, that it contained a mutton chop or a bit of bacon, would you not think that in that country something had gone wrong with the appetite for food?"[6]

But humans have long attached transcendent and poetic language to sex. From the Song of Songs to the Kama Sutra, from Shakespeare to Taylor Swift, humans have taken the ecstatic experience of sex and found it to be unique among human experiences, making it central to being human. It is little wonder, then, that the human elevation of sex in language would eventually lead to the modern concept of sexual identity. In today's culture, sex is used to tell us our true selves—to show us who we are *ultimately*. These are not simply sexual preferences or even desires. They are the way

5. James K. A. Smith, *Desiring the Kingdom: Worship, Worldview, and Cultural Formation*, Cultural Liturgies 1 (Grand Rapids: Baker Academic, 2009).
6. C. S. Lewis, *Mere Christianity* (New York: HarperCollins, 2000), 96.

we know who we are as our truest selves, to the degree that what I desire sexually tells me who I am. In such a way of thinking, my sexual identity is central to my actual identity. Other categories may also be employed in defining identity, such as gender, ethnicity, and political views. We moderns are primed to assert individualistic self-identity by these and other categories.

Sexual identity was not a familiar concept in the ancient world, but self-identity certainly was; humans have long attached their self-understanding to various markers, traditions, and movements. In first-century Palestine there were Zealots, Pharisees, and Roman apologists. There were Jews and gentiles. There were monotheists and polytheists, pagans and sorcerers. Then, as now, people identified themselves within these categories. How else might a riot break out in the amphitheater of Ephesus with people defending the honor of their goddess with cries of "Great is Artemis of the Ephesians"?

And yet in the midst of such identity-creating categories, people of different categories—some being directly opposed to one another—pursued a greater identity by following Jesus. One of the Twelve was Matthew, a tax collector who had supported his Roman colonizers and was friendly to the elite. Another of the Twelve, Judas, was likely a Zealot, believing that the Roman occupation must be ended and that the ruling class should be overthrown. On paper, Matthew and Judas were enemies. And yet, inexplicably, they submitted those identities to the greater identity of disciple. This category-defying community surprised those who encountered Jesus and his seemingly disparate group of followers. Why would assumed enemies set aside their differences to follow this rabbi?

The community continued to defy expectations, even after Jesus's ascension. By way of example, Acts 13 makes a point of mentioning the surprising diversity within the church at Antioch. We have Jews, Greeks, and Africans worshiping and serving together and then commissioning missionaries together. Within the Twelve, enemies became friends and fellow followers. Within the early church, ethnic lines disappeared under the lordship of Jesus.

In both the Twelve and the early church, Christians shifted their primary identity away from ethnicity or politics and toward the lordship of Jesus. The disparate views of the earliest believers found unity in the church; they believed that their relationships with one another as spiritual family would supersede any other claims on their lives. This is not insignificant. For a Jew to consort with a gentile, laying aside ceremonial cleanliness, they must have believed that they could find a sort of fulfillment that they could not find elsewhere. For the Zealot to set aside revolutionary aspirations of governmental overthrow in order to be part of a community must mean that they believed the messiahship of Jesus would provide a form of fulfillment more substantial than what they had previously envisioned. The examples could continue, but you can see the point. The communal effort to live in the way of Jesus was viewed by the earliest believers as more satisfactory than other options.

I am suggesting the same can be—or rather is—true with regard to sexuality. The communal life of the church, properly envisioned, gives a place for those who do not have a sexual partner to nevertheless find the deepest levels of intimacy and fulfillment by living in the way Jesus envisioned.

Let us turn, then, to Jesus's sexual vision in Matthew 19. Most readers will be familiar with this first portion. The conversation begins with Jesus answering a question about divorce but soon turns to a broader discussion of sexual ethics. Some religious leaders ask Jesus if it is permissible to divorce. He answers, "Haven't you read . . . that he who created them in the beginning made them male and female, and he also said, 'For this reason a man will leave his father and mother and be joined to his wife, and the two will become one flesh'? So they are no longer two, but one flesh. Therefore, what God has joined together, let no one separate" (Matt. 19:4–6).

Jesus's reply regarding marriage is surprising in that it seeks to prevent men from treating women in an unjust manner. In an ancient world where women often needed men for financial provision, legal legitimacy, and cultural protection, Jesus reminds his audience that marriage is intended to be lifelong in order to prevent a man from discarding his wife once her usefulness has expired. Women were commonly viewed as property in the ancient world, and sex was seen as the entitled right of a man, particularly a married man. Given Jesus's context, one might deduce it was common practice for married men to employ temple prostitutes or to forcibly demand sex. While we cannot know that for certain, we do know that the uneven social station of men and women in the ancient world put men in places of greater power—and that power likely extended to sex.

This lines up with Paul's exhortations in Ephesians 5 for men to love their wives as Christ loved the church. Christian men were not to dominate their wives, no matter what the prevailing culture might have allowed. Paul wanted men to treat women as equals in Christ—a far cry from the way some extremist religious communities behave today.

111

This power dynamic has to be informing Jesus's answer regarding divorce. Jesus mentions sex as a primary reason that the marriage relationship between husband and wife is not to be broken, because men would be able to take advantage of such a relationship in ways that most women could not. After the sexual union of marriage, there is more than simple biology happening, but rather "the two will become one flesh." This act is sacramental—more than simply human, it brings the divine into the relationship. Consequently, Jesus says, "What God has joined together, let no one separate." It is not terribly surprising, then, that the one exception Jesus provides to the breaking of the marriage covenant centers on sex as well.[7] In Matthew 19:9 Jesus says, "I tell you, whoever divorces his wife, except for sexual immorality, and marries another commits adultery." If sex is sacramental and intended as a sort of seal on the marriage covenant, it must be treated as holy and should not be violated.

The earliest Christians were known for their faithfulness in marriage. An ancient letter to a man named Diognetus described Christians this way: "They share their food but not their wives."

The word translated "sexual immorality" in verse 9 is the Greek word *porneia*. In the ancient Jewish world, *porneia* was often a sort of shorthand reference to the forbidden sexual practices of Leviticus 18. That chapter forbids things like incest, sex with a wife while she is menstruating, homosexual acts, and bestiality. The word was also regularly used to refer

---

7. Abuse is a different matter altogether. In 1 Cor. 7:15 Paul says, "But if the unbeliever leaves, let him leave. A brother or a sister is not bound in such cases. God has called you to live in peace." In this particular verse, desertion by a spouse is grounds for divorce. I believe abuse to be a form of desertion, especially in situations where family members are unsafe.

to fornication or adultery. Sexual betrayal by way of immorality is an exception for divorce, Jesus says, because the sexual relationship is central to marriage. Ideally speaking, sex is reserved for the covenant of marriage. If the husband or wife betrays that covenant sexually, it is an egregious act.

Aside from such a betrayal, Christian marriage is intended to be a lifetime covenant so that husband and wife might discover how to love another person with the sort of love that God has for us in Christ. No one knows my flaws better than my wife, Joy. She could list my problems, my shortcomings, and my sins with great detail. And yet, despite all those failures, she continues to love me and—to my great delight—remain married to me. She is a living example of the love of Jesus in my life. I cannot speak for her, but I hope she would say the same about me. While I know her flaws and her sins, I continue to love her and stay married to her.

Such love and commitment is a reflection of Christ. He knows us completely, and yet he loves us without fail. Marriage is a beautiful picture of the gospel. In the dynamic of marriage, a man and woman—both created in the image of God—work together in covenant to embody the love of God so that together they might show the unfailing love of Christ to the world.

But marriage is not the only picture of the gospel, and it is certainly not the only way sex might be used to portray love of Christ.

This is where readers may be less familiar with Jesus's sexual vision. After Jesus describes what a faithful marriage looks like, his disciples are incredulous: "If the relationship of a man with his wife is like this, it's better not to marry"

(Matt. 19:10). They have been accustomed to thinking of marriage as disposable and of sex as something to which they are entitled. Jesus, however, elevates sex within marriage.

But he is about to elevate it even further—by talking about eunuchs.

"Not everyone can accept this saying," Jesus says, "but only those to whom it has been given." Hence, this is an explicitly Christian sexual ethic. He continues, "For there are eunuchs who were born that way from their mother's womb, there are eunuchs who were made by men, and there are eunuchs who have made themselves that way because of the kingdom of heaven. The one who is able to accept it should accept it" (Matt. 19:11–12).

What does he mean?

As we've already seen, Jesus uses the image of a king and of the kingdom on a regular basis. Speaking of eunuchs, then, makes perfect sense for Jesus. In the ancient world, eunuchs were male members of the royal court. Because of their proximity to power and particularly to the queen and any concubines, eunuchs were emasculated so that they would pose no sexual threat to the king. They served the king at a high level; they also had to forgo the possibility of sexual relationships. Although not confirmed in the Scripture, some have theorized that Israelites exiled in Babylon—like Daniel and his friends—would have been made eunuchs in their service to the Babylonian king.

When the disciples are taken aback at the fact that marriage is more serious than they initially understood and that sex is not something to be assumed, Jesus gives a simple response:

You don't have to have sex to live a fulfilled life. You can simply serve the King.

There are some, Jesus says, who are born with a body that does not allow them to have sex. There are some whose bodies were altered to become literal eunuchs. And there are some who chose to live as metaphorical eunuchs through celibacy for the kingdom of God. Long before the ideas of sexual orientation or sexual identity, Jesus suggested something radical—a group of people who chose to forgo sex so that they might focus on serving the Lord.

The stunning kingdom reality is quite direct in this passage: sex is not ultimate. I remember a young man coming to me at one point after I had preached a sermon on the return of Christ. He made a comment: "I am excited about Jesus returning one day to set all things right, but I hope it happens after I get married." He grinned sheepishly. I understood what was in his mind; he would hate to miss out on the ecstasy of sex. I replied, "I imagine the pleasure we will experience in union with Christ will be greater than any pleasure we will experience in this world."

I absolutely believed that to be true. But I also realized my flaw; I had not communicated that belief very well to my congregation. We have made sex out to be the pinnacle of human existence and, by extension, have unintentionally communicated that a life without sex is a life that is not fulfilling.

We do not do this with other human experiences. We do not believe that eating a particular dish or visiting a particular city makes a life ultimately successful. I love good food and enjoy travel. Who doesn't? But I would never believe that if I lived my life without having tasted, say, a perfectly prepared crème brûlée, that I would have somehow lived a fruitless life. The flavor of dessert is good, but it is not ultimate. Jesus alone is ultimate. Seeing Paris might be a great gift to enjoy, but I believe I will enjoy better gifts in the new heavens and new earth. Our American sensibilities tend to make sex something more than it is, when our Christian community ought to point to Jesus alone as that which satisfies.

So why do we often think and act as if sex—or sexual orientation or sexual identity—is ultimate?

I mentioned earlier that marriage is one of the ways Christians can faithfully portray love of Christ in relation to sex. Jesus tells us another way forward here: to forgo sex completely in service of the King. Most of us living in the modern world are almost unable to consider such an option, particularly given the way sex is given center stage in entertainment venues of every sort. A sexless relationship—particularly one with a member of the opposite sex—is not meaningful. A close friendship—even with a member of the same sex—while viewed as good, is rarely seen as something that can sustain people. Almost to a fault, popular culture (along with many in the church) has lost the ability to imagine relational satisfaction apart from sex.

But Christians have envisioned a possible life without sex from their very beginnings. Evangelicalism has been obsessed with marriage and kids for much of its brief history—sometimes to a point that it made marriage and kids appear to be ultimate, mirroring rather than challenging the prevailing culture. I recall a time when some of the single adults in my congregation asked me to consider their perspective when writing a sermon or offering pastoral care. I was a much younger pastor at the time, and they had identified a blind spot in my theology—a theology I had picked up in my time within evangelicalism. From "ring by spring" pressure to find a mate for Christian college seniors to countless books and seminars on marriage to the Quiverfull movement to

have as many children as possible in order to influence culture, I had been overtly taught that marriage and kids were
the best way to live as a Christian.

But that certainly isn't what the New Testament says.
Yes, the Scriptures give patterns of living for husbands and
wives, but singleness and celibacy are live options given to
the earliest believers in the church and ought to be taught
as such today.

Jesus—our supreme example—never married.

Paul—the most well-known church planter and mission-
ary of all time—was not married.

The apostles went to the ends of the known world to proclaim the good news of Jesus and his kingdom—many of
them presumably without additional commitment to a wife.

As best I can tell, Paul took Jesus's words in Matthew 19
to mean that not being married was a good thing—perhaps
even preferable to being married—for service to the kingdom. In 1 Corinthians 7 we see that sex and singleness was a
topic of conversation in the church at Corinth. Paul says married couples ought to have sex in order to prevent temptation,
but in verses 7–8 he gives this straightforward advice: "I wish
that all people were as I am. . . . I say to the unmarried and
to widows: It is good for them if they remain as I am." Paul
gets straight to the point: he would prefer them to remain
unmarried and celibate. He explains his reasoning in verses
32–34: "I want you to be without concerns. The unmarried
man is concerned about the things of the Lord—how he may
please the Lord. But the married man is concerned about
the things of the world—how he may please his wife—and
his interests are divided. The unmarried woman or virgin
is concerned about the things of the Lord, so that she may
be holy both in body and in spirit. But the married woman

is concerned about the things of the world—how she may please her husband."

Paul is clear: given the choice, he thinks it is better to remain unmarried and celibate. But he is careful to explain that this is not a requirement. Instead, it is for those who can choose this life. "I am saying this for your own benefit, not to put a restraint on you, but to promote what is proper and so that you may be devoted to the Lord without distraction" (1 Cor. 7:35). Paul and Jesus are in agreement here. Marriage and sex are good, but celibacy is also a faithful and good way to live. For Paul, it seemed to be the preferred way to live.

The knowledge of sex not being ultimate is also good news to married couples. One of the quiet promises of purity teaching was that if one waited until marriage for sex, they would have "mind-blowing" sex within marriage. If the couples I have counseled over the years are any indication, that quiet promise has been left unfulfilled many times over. What a relief for couples to know that they can find a way forward sexually without having to feel the pressure of sexual performance! For the man with erectile dysfunction or the woman who experiences pain during sex, knowing that sex is simply one aspect of marriage rather than the ultimate expression of marriage can be freeing—and can turn us toward hope in union with Christ.

It is incumbent on the church to revive teachings of celibacy alongside teaching that sex is to be reserved within the covenant of marriage. If Jesus and Paul modeled this life, and if they both teach its viability within the faith, we ought to do the same. I cannot help but wonder if our tendency within evangelical churches to ignore or undervalue celibacy is because we secretly believe the modern narrative of the ultimacy of sex. I certainly taught as much earlier in my ministry. I imagine many others have as well.

Zena Hitz cuts through the fog of such thinking: "We act as if life without sex is impossible, and entertain the thought, even if less commonly nowadays than in my youth, that sex with strangers is harmless. Both cannot be true: Either sex reaches down to the core of our being, and so ought be treated with reverence and caution, as something which might bear life's meaning for us, or it is harmless, like chewing bubble gum, and can be given up without a second thought."[8]

Hitz is, I think, correct. We must decide. If sex is indeed important, then we must guard it. If it is meaningless, then we can give it up. Those of us who call ourselves Christian can find meaning, ecstasy, and pleasure in union with Christ. I am encouraged by stories of those who submitted their sexual desires to their life of following Jesus—whether by marriage or by celibacy. I think the very real option of celibacy gives hope for those who have been so traumatized by past abuse, specifically sexual abuse, that they yearn for a life in which they might experience deep love and knowledge without believing they are somehow living a lesser form of obedience to Jesus, or a less meaningful life than married people.

What might it look like for a church to encourage both marriage and celibacy as viable ways of sexual faithfulness? Plenty of churches have premarital counseling, courses for nearlyweds and newlyweds, marriage enrichment seminars, and the like. Perhaps churches could also intentionally teach and disciple those who live without sex. Perhaps we might venerate those who give their time and lives more fully to the

8. Zena Hitz, *A Philosopher Looks at the Religious Life* (New York: Cambridge University Press, 2023), 121.

call of the gospel precisely because they do not have a spouse. Perhaps we might arrange ways for single church members to be grafted into other family units more intentionally— through dinners and gatherings. Perhaps we might teach hospitality in such a way that no church member would ever feel as if he or she was incapable of knowing true emotional and spiritual intimacy. Perhaps we might help cultivate a deep belonging among our single and celibate adults in a way that models the New Testament picture of spiritual family. The church I pastor has done some of these well. In other areas we are woefully inadequate. I believe we can improve.

A church that does these things offers a new way of thinking about sex, celibacy, self-denial, hospitality, and spiritual family.

This sort of thinking can give great hope to those of us who fight against sexual desires in our bodies that often seem stronger than the Spirit within us. I use "us" intentionally. I know what it is like to have sexual desires that fall outside the image of covenant marriage that I uphold and have committed myself to. The fact that those thoughts and desires still arise in my heart allows me to better understand and empathize with my friends who have different sexual desires. Rather than finding myself judging them, I recognize that the battle against our desires is real and must be taken seriously. This recognition inspires me to envision a more robust form of church community where celibacy can be celebrated and supported.

The human heart can rationalize most any sexual desire or behavior given enough time, but most people would agree there must be some line that cannot be crossed. In today's culture, that line is pedophilia, but even that line is being challenged in small segments of the population. We need boundaries for sexuality, for without them we damage human flourishing. The boundaries given by Jesus and the New Testament are our best path forward, for they remind us that sex is good, but it is not everything.

These boundaries are not easy to accept, however. I can envision the looks on the faces of the disciples as Jesus concludes this radical teaching. You can almost hear them thinking, "Give up sex? Is he serious? How would I ever have a family? Aren't I supposed to have children, to be fruitful and multiply?"

And then, as if on cue, a group of parents arrive with their kids, asking Jesus to bless them. Perhaps the disciples are a bit grumpy from what Jesus has just taught; perhaps they think Jesus too important to interact with kids. Whatever the case, they move to send the children away. But Jesus rebukes them, welcomes the kids, and then says to the disciples, "Leave the little children alone, and don't try to keep them from coming to me, because the kingdom of heaven belongs to such as these" (Matt. 19:14).

In this, Jesus reminds his disciples that their progeny is not limited to biological children they may have but includes those who may come into the kingdom. This, of course, is a continuation of what Jesus has already said in speaking of the kingdom as a family in Matthew 12:49–50. He says, "Here are my mother and my brothers! For whoever does the will of my Father in heaven is my brother and sister and mother."

This language of the kingdom as a family continues in the New Testament. The earliest Christians were asked to relate to one another as family, as brothers and sisters. Even today many Christians address one another as "brother" and "sister." The church of the kingdom is intended to serve as a family, especially for those who may choose to forgo marriage and sex.

Such a vision, however, will require recapturing hospitality, a practice in which the earliest Christians excelled. If Christians were known for loving their enemies (as discussed in chap. 4), they were also known for their deep love for one another, as evidenced in their material generosity and the way their communities operated as extended families. The New Testament asks for believers to practice the opposite of xenophobia (fear of strangers) when describing how to treat others. Scripture uses the Greek word *philoxenoi*; literally translated, it means "the love of strangers." This is the New Testament vision of hospitality.

Those who have no family or community will find acceptance where they are loved for who they are. Sadly, while churches have often taught sexual ethics, they have less often lived out hospitality and have pushed out those who have non-conforming sexual desires. It is a great irony that the group of people often obsessed with marriage and family have ostracized those most in need of a family. We must come to recognize the different types of people and different situations that exist within our congregations, and we must extend the offer of family without qualification or stigma. If we will not offer the intimacy of family, how could we ever fault people for finding that needed intimacy elsewhere?

How can we ask people to forgo marriage and sex if we will not live as family to them? Church must welcome everyone—and not simply into a church service. Church must welcome believers to both the Table and also to our respective kitchen tables. We must share Communion *and* coffee. Somehow, Communion wafers and coffee saucers become spiritual weapons against our various internal darknesses when we gather. And we wield those spiritual weapons best when we battle together—confessing our sins, seeking to be both known and accepted, no matter who we are.

Jesus knew exactly what he was doing as he envisioned the kingdom as a hospitable family. He knew that a radical commitment to the King would require a radical reimagination of family. He knew we would need to be brothers and sisters to one another. He knew we would need to have deep friendships. He knew we would need, in the words of Hitz, to have the combination of "deep exposure and deep acceptance."[9]

This is the way forward for sexual healing—a place where sex is important but not ultimate, a place where those who are not married can find family, a place where those who are celibate do not have to live in secret or as outcasts but are welcomed at the table as brothers and sisters. If Hitz is correct, we can indeed submit our sexual desires to the lordship of Jesus, and we can do so without losing a meaningful life.

Some family is welcomed through the covenant of marriage. Other family is welcomed through the covenant of the gospel.

Sexual healing comes when we see one another not as objects of desire but as brothers and sisters worthy of love.

Sexual healing comes when we share our lives with others. By this everyone is enriched.

---

9. Hitz, *A Philosopher Looks at the Religious Life*, 122.

7

God and Country

Jesus on Politics

Otherworldliness and secularism are simply two sides of the same coin—namely, the lack of belief in God's kingdom.

—Dietrich Bonhoeffer, "Thy Kingdom Come!"

"My kingdom is not of this world," said Jesus.

—John 18:36

I have not had the best of luck with politicians while serving as a pastor. Once I invited a local politician to share his faith story on a Sunday morning. Despite agreeing not to do so, he used our pulpit instead to deliver a stump speech, which caused multiple families to leave our church. On another occasion I invited a different politician so that we could pray for his upcoming initiative designed to reduce homelessness. His particular party affiliation concerned and offended some to the point that they too left the church. Like I said: not the best of luck.

I felt confident with my decision in each case beforehand, and in both cases I learned that attempting to overlap Christianity and political action is far more complex than a much younger version of myself understood. Personally, I've always been interested in politics and its relationship to faith, but any attempt I've made to connect pastoral ministry to politics hasn't gone as envisioned. I have learned that when you mix the church and politics, you usually get politics, even if you are trying hard to avoid them. This is, in part, because the politics of the state and the politics of the kingdom have different goals but also because those within the church carry competing visions of how the state ought to operate. Even the best of intentions can be misinterpreted or misunderstood when these competing visions of statecraft come into play.

Since those incidents, I've rethought my approach to politics, particularly the way the church and politics ought to relate to each other. With these competing visions of the state present within the church, I began to re-examine how Jesus approached the ruling powers of his day. I outline some of those thoughts in this chapter. This is less political theory and more a pastoral vision of how a congregation might interact with the powers that be in a way that is simultaneously faithful, prophetic, and participatory. I've already detailed some of the dangers Christians face with regard to the political realm in my chapter on power and service, but the world requires leaders and administrators for things to operate properly. The vast majority of us will never run for or serve in public office, yet we must live within the political system of our respective nations. Others of us will indeed serve as elected officials. Both the believer who is elected and the citizen congregant must navigate the relationship between church and politics. Consequently, we must think about our individual and congregational responsibilities in politics while specifically considering our faith.[1]

To put it succinctly, the two most important things Christians can do politically—in my opinion—are to tell the truth and to live faithfully as the people of God. When we do those two things, we portray the kingdom, and we make it possible to envision a different way of being altogether. There is, however, a third piece of this political vision. Christians should also participate in the civic life of the nation in a way that faithfully models the way of Jesus in the world. These three things: prophetic speech, embodied community, and participation are the ways I see Jesus engaging the politics of his day and, by extension, showing us how to move forward.

I cannot say that this vision will necessarily bring about overarching or systemic change. Others have thought much more deeply about what would be necessary for such a wholesale change to take place. This vision is pastoral in that it is local and possible for each of us to join. It focuses not only on crafting a life-giving alternative community but also argues that if our only political strategy is one of creating an alternative community, we might unintentionally abandon our greater communities—the very ones where we are intended to bring life. We must fashion the church as an alternative to the state, but we must also devise ways to take part.

1. There are any number of excellent political theologians and practitioners who have thought about this on a much deeper level than I will ever be able to approach in a single chapter. I will recommend a few specifically: William T. Cavanaugh and Graham Ward are academics who have done excellent work in recent years. Kaitlyn Schiess and Michael Wear write for a more popular audience and provide clear Christian thinking on these topics as well.

The Christian imagination has been concerned with politics from its very beginning. That concern has continued and ripened over the years, bringing many Christians to produce fruitful (and extensive) theological and political theories. From the apostle Paul's exhortations to respect our rulers in Romans 13 to Augustine's magnum opus, *The City of God*, the earliest Christians wrestled with how a community could faithfully embody the commands of Jesus and proclaim his gospel while living in a society ruled by a government with a completely different perspective. Successive generations have done the same. Thinkers as diverse as Thomas Müntzer and Abraham Kuyper (and countless others) have wondered and argued how the church and politics ought to coexist.

Looking through the lens of cooperation and collaboration, I believe a pastoral political vision will focus on creating a healthy church while addressing the systems that affect the city in which the church is situated. It is thus a contextual vision. I live in a democratic republic; our opportunity for political engagement is different from someone living in, say, a dictatorship. Nevertheless, local, popular political will exists in all contexts, no matter the system of government, meaning that churches can find ways to bring about positive community change.

Jesus's use of kingdom terminology was intentional. Modern Americans thing in terms of presidents, but those in Jesus's day thought in terms of kings. Kings wield authority and demand allegiance. By describing his vision of following God as a kingdom, Jesus held it in direct contrast to the rule of Caesar. His contemporaries gathered as much; he was called "the king of the Jews" on the day of his crucifixion, even if that title was given in mockery. The people tried to make him king more than once; they waved palm branches when he entered Jerusalem as if he were a conquering king. In contrast, to distance themselves from Jesus, the crowds assembled before Pilate cried, "We have no king but Caesar!" (John 19:15).

Jesus knew exactly what he was doing with his words.

Once, the religious leaders of the day came to Jesus to test the boundaries of this kingdom he envisioned in relation to the earthly kingdom of Caesar. They were likely hoping to catch Jesus in an act of treason, thereby warranting his arrest. They couched their question in simple terms: "Is it lawful to pay taxes to Caesar or not?" (Matt. 22:17). If Jesus said that they should pay taxes, they would reveal him to be a traitor to his own people. If, instead, he said they should not pay taxes, they could turn him over to the Roman authorities as one who taught treason against Caesar.

Jesus's reply was brilliant—so brilliant that it continues to amaze two thousand years later. He asked for a coin. Holding it up, he asked, "Whose image and inscription is this?" When they told him it had Caesar's inscription, he gave his political philosophy in the simplest of terms: "Give, then, to Caesar the things that are Caesar's, and to God the things that are God's" (Matt. 22:20–21).

What do we gather from Jesus's teaching? There are certain areas where we may be required to support earthly authorities—taxes, for example. There are other areas where our allegiance to the Lord may run counter to our allegiance to the government. In those instances, we should first give God our allegiance. Simply put, Christians are to support the earthly king when possible, but if there is a conflict, our primary allegiance is to God. More simply put, support the king, but seek God's kingdom first.

This political philosophy seems to have made an impact on the earliest disciples. Decades later, the apostle Paul wrote to the church in Rome, the seat of Caesar's power. The believers there were dealing with some of the same questions, including how to navigate the political waters of the day when they did not recognize God's authority. Paul gave a similar response to that of Jesus, taking it a bit further: "Let everyone submit to the governing authorities, since there is no authority except from God, and the authorities that exist are instituted by God" (Rom. 13:1). The Christian's primary calling is not to overturn governmental systems but rather to give primary allegiance to King Jesus. In doing that, Paul says, the authorities will see the good of the faith.

This philosophy made perfect sense in a government filled with pagans who were unfamiliar with Jesus. Paul's philosophy gave Christians protection; in doing good, the church flew under the radar and avoided detection and potential persecution. But what about now, when the West has been won over by Christian ways of thinking, even if those ways of thinking are not broadly recognized? Should the church choose relative obscurity? Or is there another way to consider giving both Caesar and God that which they are owed?

Christian civic involvement begins with the rightful recognition that the church's first obligation in politics is to tell the truth. Christians tell the truth in their communities by proclaiming the gospel of Jesus and living the truth within their congregations. They also tell the truth by advocating for honesty within the public square. By choosing this sort of faithful truth-telling, the church embodies that which both Jesus and Paul envisioned—not a community seeking to overthrow the government, but a community envisioning a healthier, more collaborative and cooperative alternative, a place where people are formed into the image of Jesus.

At the same time, these potential communities of human cooperation, collaboration, and flourishing will exist in the midst of a state operating under a different set of principles. To complicate matters further, several of those serving in elected positions will claim to be Christians but may or may not pursue policies that foster a kingdom vision. The church, then, needs a way to honor the king while faithfully representing God's kingdom.

In the American form of government, citizens are expected to speak into the public square, so Christians should do so. But Christians, like other groups in the West, recognize that they are one voice in a pluralistic space. Consequently, concerns must be voiced in a way that is true to the kingdom and also respectful of the competing visions of others. This is, to put it mildly, a delicate matter. Christians must honor their rulers, obey Jesus, give congregants a positive political vision, and somehow exhort politicians who are Christian believers to walk out their faith—all while doing so in a way that is not perceived as religious overreach. What's a church to do?

In part, the political vision of the church lies in creating an alternative political reality by faithfully living as a community. Many Anabaptist communities—like the Bruderhof—have lived this sort of reality for some time. The philosophy is straightforward enough: by living in community in a distinct way, we demonstrate a different way to live that creates a different political reality within the church. Theologian Stanley Hauerwas gave great credence to such thinking, often arguing that the best thing the church could do was to simply *be the church*.[2] To be sure, faithful communal living is an excellent public witness, but many critics of such communal thinking rightly point out one flaw: while living as community is life-giving within the church, it does little to effect change in the world outside the community, particularly when circumstances outside the community are harmful to the greater good. What can the church do in order to maintain its faithfulness while also working to promote the good?

The prophetic tradition of the Black church charts one path forward for civic engagement. Martin Luther King Jr. once said that the church is the conscience of the state.[3] By this he meant that in the political realm, the church's duty is often the faithful proclamation of truth to power in defense of those who are poor, those who are weak, and those who are unable to have a voice. For shorthand, I'm going to call such proclamation of truth by the name of prophecy. In common usage, the word "prophecy" indicates predicting the future. But the prophecy I'm speaking of has nothing to do with soothsaying. This sort of prophecy is about having the courage to speak about the concerns of Jesus in the corridors of power, particularly when such a message may not be popular.

If the church is to be the conscience of the state, it must begin with the courage to tell the truth, because those in power are often seduced by the pragmatic and the expedient.

2. There are any number of Hauerwas's works one could consult to better understand his theological vision. He is arguably the most influential theologian of his generation. A good place to start is Stanley Hauerwas, *A Community of Character: Toward a Constructive Christian Social Ethic* (South Bend, IN: Notre Dame University Press, 1991).

3. Martin Luther King Jr., "A Knock at Midnight," sermon preached between July 1, 1962, and March 31, 1963, most likely in Atlanta, Georgia, according to The Martin Luther King Jr. Research and Education Institute at Stanford University.

Governments need to get things done. The church should help them get the right things done and done in an honorable way. Sometimes, however, in the name of getting things done, we can forget our identity.

Long before there was a church, God designed the prophetic relationship to those in power. When in 1 Samuel the people of Israel decide they no longer want to be led only by the Lord but instead want to be like other nations, they call on Samuel to give them an earthly king. Samuel is angry about their request, but the Lord answers their desire—with one small tweak: each king must have a prophet. Both are needed, because without the accountability of the prophet, the king will have no limitation and therefore will likely misuse his power.

Consider just a few of the confrontations between prophets and kings in the Bible. Nathan confronts David about his infidelity with Bathsheba. Samuel confronts Saul about consulting a medium instead of the Lord. Elijah confronts Ahab about Ba'al worship.

Over and over, the role of the prophet was to confront the king, to tell the king when pragmatism or power had corrupted the Lord's vision to make Israel a distinct people. The prophet was the one appointed by God to prophesy with truth, to push back against the allure of power, to moor the kingdom of Israel to the pier of God's design for it. The prophet's job is straightforward: Be the Lord's representative to the king. Speak the Lord's words to the king. Inquire of the Lord on behalf of the king.

In short, the prophet is to make certain that the king follows God's plan and governs in line with what the Lord wants. If the king doesn't do this, the prophet's job is to speak directly to the king and instruct him to bring his actions back in line with God's plan. This is what Samuel does with Saul, what Nathan does with David, and what Elijah does with Ahab. The prophet must maintain a holy distance so that truth can be spoken without being compromised by power.

In Scripture, when Israel has a king, they always have a prophet, because no one individual serves as both prophet and king. This is essential, because it indicates that even the best of kings and the best of prophets are not suited to hold both offices simultaneously. One office is designed to hold the other in check. Israel believed in checks and balances long before the United States had three branches of federal government.

I believe this sort of prophetic model is the best way to embody Jesus's political philosophy in a democratic republic. In this model, the church serves as the prophet to those believers who choose to occupy the kingly world of politics. Those believers who serve in the political realm must fight the seductions of power, so they will require a faithful church who will speak clearly about the kingdom and its overlap with the public sphere. We speak clearly when we faithfully and communally embody the way of Jesus, when we faithfully proclaim the Word in that community, and when we work toward a Christian vision of life within the public square.

The relationship between the prophets and kings of Israel reminds us that truth can speak to power only when it is separate, when it is on the outside, when it has a healthy distance.

Distance, of course, is not always easy to measure or to maintain. History is filled with examples of pastors struggling to maintain distance from power. One example from my own tradition: In the 1850s and 1860s (and beyond) a host of Southern pastors preached on the virtues of slavery.

My childhood denomination, Southern Baptists, began inauspiciously as a slave-approving alternative to Northern Baptists. In the 1960s you could find plenty of pastors in the South supporting "separate but equal" policies. Why? The power structures in the communities of the South supported slavery in the 1860s and segregation in the 1960s. Any pastor who spoke in favor of abolition or desegregation would be without a job.

The prophet was not able to hold the king in check. This is what happens when those who are supposed to be prophetic are in too close a relationship with those in power.

It is one thing to be charged with the responsibility of serving as the conscience of the state. It is quite another thing to actually do it. In a situation where speaking truth to a congregation or a president might lead to job loss, family discomfort, and social awkwardness, it is often easier to not speak truth to power, even if it is simply congregational power. In fact, it is profoundly easier to say what those in power want to hear. It is easier because it allows us to stay close to those in power, be it those who control our jobs or those who govern.

Our nation has a long history of pastors and politicians working in close proximity.[4] While there have been moments when this has worked out well, the closeness of pastors and politicians has certainly been too cozy at times. It is good to be a "spiritual adviser" to someone in power, as long as

---

4. Almost every American president has had at least one pastor as a spiritual adviser. Many of these advisers are anonymous in history because they did not seek the spotlight. Most recently, I am thinking of one of my mentors who has been in the Oval Office many times but has never been photographed with the president. His words: "I go in through the back door and leave through the back door. My job is to give counsel and pray, not to have my picture taken."

one can keep a healthy distance and retain the ability to be prophetic. But as our history details, it is difficult to stay in the role of spiritual advisor once one has entered the corridors of power.

It is thrilling to be invited into the king's court. And it is tempting to say whatever is necessary in order to stay there. Once you have been privy to decision-making, to personal favors, and to influential relationships, it is difficult to hold the line on being prophetic. If you tell those in power that they are acting in a way that is unethical or marginalizing those who are downtrodden, they likely won't respond well. If you say those things in a public forum? You'll probably lose any access to those in power. Being the conscience of the state comes at a cost, and that cost is usually one of comfort.

As the National Socialist Party was coming to power in the 1930s, Dietrich Bonhoeffer and several other pastors in Germany looked for active ways to resist. Just before this, Bonhoeffer had lived among the African American church in Harlem and had seen how faith in Jesus could be used to both sustain those without power and give courage to speak to those in power. During his time in New York, Bonhoeffer attended Abyssinian Baptist Church, pastored by Adam Clayton Powell. Powell was a community giant who leveraged the influence of Abyssinian to make a difference. The Great Depression had ravaged the economy of Harlem, and Powell sought to care for those in need through his church's ministry. Each Sunday, Bonhoeffer heard the gospel preached, but he also saw how the church might speak up and speak for those who did not have a voice in the community.[5]

5. Reggie Williams, in *Bonhoeffer's Black Jesus: Harlem Renaissance Theology and an Ethic of Resistance* (Waco: Baylor University Press, 2014), does a masterful job of exploring the Black church's influence on the young Bonhoeffer.

Bonhoeffer was deeply influenced by his time in Harlem and particularly by the Black church. The influence became increasingly apparent on his return to Berlin, as he considered the church's responsibility of engagement with the powers in Germany. On the day after Adolf Hitler became the Reich chancellor, Bonhoeffer gave a radio address criticizing the notion of a führer—an all-powerful leader. It was an incredibly brave move that led the radio station to cut off his address mid-broadcast. Bonhoeffer and other members of the so-called Confessing Church refused to allow their churches to be co-opted by the Nazis. Instead of situating their theology within their national identity, they chose to situate their identity within the lordship of Jesus. They founded underground seminaries to train pastors who would oppose führer theology; they preached the gospel and the Bible faithfully against authoritarian power; they wrote and taught how the theology of the New Testament opposed the policies of the Nazi government. Bonhoeffer's classic book *The Cost of Discipleship* (*Nachfolge*) was written to resist führer theology and instead highlight the lordship of Jesus.

Bonhoeffer and other Confessing Church members understood that when the government was exercising unhealthy power, a primary responsibility of the church was to resist through proclamation of the Scriptures that portrayed a way of life faithful to the kingdom. They saw themselves as prophets who were charged to speak truth to the king—even if the king was not listening. Confessing Christians believed such faithful reading of Scripture, solid theology, and powerful preaching centering on the lordship of Jesus would be one part of countering a government bent on upholding a cult of personality.

Bonhoeffer reminds us that prophetic resistance is useful, good, and faithful.

***

Twice in the New Testament the church receives a positive command to resist. Both times, the command is given to resist the devil: "Resist the devil, and he will flee from you" (James 4:7). "Resist him, firm in the faith, knowing that the same kind of sufferings are being experienced by your fellow believers throughout the world" (1 Pet. 5:9).

Is the government—local or otherwise—leading an agenda or promoting a policy that is in clear opposition to Scripture? That is, is it clearly evil? If so, it is good to resist with teaching and theology and preaching and practice. Yes, we need to use the right tone. Yes, we need to be mindful of outsiders. Yes, we should employ grace and love as best we can. And, yes, we are to submit to our rulers as Romans 13 commands us to do.

But truth must be spoken. The witness must be lived. The church must model an alternative.

So we speak up about actions and policies that are contrary to God's cooperative and collaborative vision of human flourishing. In some ways, our calls will sound familiar. Evangelicals continue to express concern, for example, about the moral problems surrounding abortion, particularly elective late-term abortion. At the same time, the church needs to find its prophetic voice in spaces Western evangelicals have historically or lately been silent. We should speak out against the blatant racism still rampant in many of our cities, and we should consider how to repair the divide.[6] We should

6. As just one example of this disparity, a friend in Chattanooga shared the results of a federal study where the two largest banks in the area granted Black Americans a total of four conventional home loans in a four-year period

cry out against corruption and ill-gotten gains both within politics and within the often unethical relationship between corporations and politicians. Why does the average net worth of high-level politicians increase so dramatically while they are in office?[7] We ought to defend the immigrant and the stranger, just as Scripture exhorts believers to do, while simultaneously working for border security and full-scale immigration reform. We ought to cry out and plead the case of the poor, both through immediate financial assistance and through longer-term programs that can address root issues causing poverty. We ought to do these things, not to be immovable cultural obstacles, but to be faithful to the kingdom Jesus envisioned.

Careful readers will note that the kingdom vision of political issues does not cleanly square with the talking points of either of the main political parties in the United States or of many political parties anywhere in the world. Those of us who claim a kingdom vision for politics will invariably feel passionate about issues but rarely at home in the traditional political confines afforded by culture. Instead, we prophesy and cast vision. To be honest, a kingdom vision of politics will not always provide a clear candidate to vote for in an election. Christians should, in my opinion, study the available candidates and their stances on major issues, pray, and then follow the leading of the Spirit.

(2011–14). See appendix B in the following report, "Whose Reinvestment? The Failures of Equitable Home Lending in Chattanooga," Chattanooga Organized for Action, 2016, https://www.chattaction.org/uploads/9/4/5/1/94512373 /bank_report_final_with_appendices.pdf.

7. Sarah Rosier and the Congress team, "Changes in Net Worth of U.S. Senators and Representatives (Personal Gain Index," Ballotpedia, July 24, 2014, https://ballotpedia.org/Changes_in_Net_Worth_of_U.S._Senators_and _Representatives_(Personal_Gain_Index).

Between elections, they should actively engage to speak and organize prophetically to make the world look a little more like heaven. I believe in strengthening our civic institutions through involvement and participation, including Christians serving in political office—as long as those serving in office are able to be faithfully prophetic at the appropriate times as the Spirit leads.

We ought to prophesy because we envision a world of cooperation and collaboration where all are able to flourish in a kingdom vision. Prophetic resistance is faithful when grounded in Jesus's vision of the kingdom, because it is intended not simply to tear down that which exists but to cast a vision for that which might be.

Why was Martin Luther King Jr.'s "I Have A Dream" speech so effective? When he stood on the steps of the National Mall and decried the racist structures and attitudes infecting much of the United States at that time, he spoke directly to the halls of power, crying out for justice. Why was his speech so memorable? Why did it move the hearts of many in our nation? His most famous speech was a seeming public paradox. He issued a public rebuke, but he also managed to sway many hearts. How could he do both at the same time?

There are many reasons, to be sure, but Dr. King was effective, at least partly, because he did not only rebuke. He also envisioned the kingdom of God. He imagined a new way of life. And he described it to his hearers. Armed with a new way to see the world, Dr. King did not solely shame those who had been entrenched in bigotry; he gave them permission to move in a different direction.

I hear some version of this statement regularly: "The world knows what Christians are against, but it does not know what they are for."

To be honest, I can't help but wonder at times if Christians themselves know what they are for. I chalk this up to a basic issue: we do not envision, imagine, and embody the kingdom of God nearly enough. We cannot advocate for particular policies if we do not have a clear vision of what, precisely, the kingdom looks like.

When Jesus came, he proclaimed the good news of the kingdom of God. He declared that the kingdom of God was "at hand." In other words, he preached that one could live as if Jesus was King in the present. Those who followed Jesus not only accepted the promise of eternal life by following the Messiah, they also submitted to his teaching—also called his yoke (Matt 11:29–30). The two cannot be separated. You cannot accept the truth that Jesus is the Son of God, the long-awaited Messiah, and then reject his teachings. His teachings are the description of his kingdom—the way he will rule into eternity and the way his church will live in the here and now. Jesus's incarnation, death, and resurrection are the gospel of salvation, and the teachings of Jesus are the outline of the kingdom.

This is what the Sermon on the Mount is: a description of how life is under the rule and reign of King Jesus. "You have heard it said," Jesus declares, "but I say to you." The old ways and the kingdom ways aren't synonymous. The kingdom pushes things deeper—to a heart level.

The kingdom is the outworking of the gospel. It is the way that those who have been saved by Jesus live. It is the redemptive end goal. It is what the world will one day be when it is finally and completely redeemed by Jesus's glorious return. Until then, it is best seen in the way those who declare allegiance to Jesus live.

The kingdom of God is the gospel of God made alive by the people of God.

If the kingdom of God is this essential, it must be the centerpiece of the church's political philosophy. The kingdom is the church's answer for the world's political posturing. When the world scrambles toward violence and retribution, the church should present the kingdom as a viable alternative.

But to do that, the church must understand the kingdom. It must love the kingdom. And to do that, it must consistently imagine, proclaim, and embody what kingdom life looks like.

If we only rebuke, if we only resist, we provide only a negative view of our Lord. The kingdom is the positive way forward. It is the way of explaining what we are for. It is the thing Christians can point to when they want to contrast the way of Jesus with the way of the world.

That is exactly what Bonhoeffer did when he wrote *The Cost of Discipleship*. Although best known for its opening chapter on "cheap grace," the book is a full-orbed treatment of Matthew's gospel, focusing on the Sermon on the Mount. In chapter after chapter, Bonhoeffer lays out what the kingdom of God looks like—according to the teachings of Jesus. Bonhoeffer used the work as a textbook as he trained Confessing Church pastors in illegal seminaries.

Those of us who hope the church will move beyond simply rebuking and resisting need to present real-life substance to our hopes. Jesus is clear: the kingdom is the way forward, and it is what ought to consume our imaginations.

Pastors and church leaders ought to consistently teach, envision, and embody kingdom values for their church because a rebuke without an alternative vision is mere theory. As Bonhoeffer understood, however, when you live out the kingdom as it is portrayed in the New Testament—particularly the Sermon on the Mount—it becomes a tangible example for others to observe. It creates a reality for which the church might yearn.

So should we rebuke? Of course. But we cannot stop there. We must surrender to the kingdom and allow it to shape our thinking, our proclamation, and our church life. We must allow it to be the driving force behind our politics—not a particular party or candidate. We must continually be the people urging our own national politicians to shape our nation to look increasingly like the kingdom.

Beyond that, we can—and should—organize to help bring out kingdom living in our respective communities. A Christian political theory that is only prophetic speech will fall short of the kingdom vision. Action must be taken on behalf of the community. For example, if hunger or education is problematic in a community or in a state, Christians should speak up in order to ensure that those in the community have opportunity for provision and care. As mentioned in the previous chapter on money and possessions, one of the long-standing causes of the church has been the care of the poor. One way we care for the poor is through generosity.

Another way is to advocate politically for those who may have less of a voice or a constituency within the corridors of power. Much of the Christian political vision will involve supporting policies and politicians who will work for the benefit of all citizens, particularly those who are vulnerable and politically weak. Most political processes center on the preservation of power. Christian politics ought to work not only to speak the truth but to also craft a reality that cares for our weaker neighbors, that creates a space for them in the community. As we stand for the weak, we turn neighbor love into political action.

As I write, there is a move among some Christians to envision a form of politics that is not an alternative or corrective to the power structures of the day but rather an attempt to replace those powers with a distinctly theocratic vision. This political vision, popularly known as Christian nationalism, has gained traction among some evangelicals for its insistence on a narrow and more explicitly Christian vision for the United States. To be clear, Christian nationalism is not the participation of Christians within the public square, nor is it Christians advocating for particular policies from their perspective. Christian nationalism—as I understand it—usually works to institute Christianity as an official state religion and legislate toward those ends. This may initially sound good in theory, but experience reveals something different altogether. The values of Christian nationalism are more frequently self-serving than they are about the public good.

While I completely agree that the church should influence governance toward the kingdom, history teaches us that when the church and government are too closely related, the witness of the church is almost always corrupted and the spiritual health of the corresponding nation struggles. History is filled with examples of such corruption and struggle, both ancient and modern. We need only look at the German church in the 1930s to see the outcome when a nationalized religion is intertwined with political power.

Further, the Christian nationalism to which I am referring eschews philosophical and cultural diversity and instead opts for a more strongly formed and held Christian state to the exclusion of others, becoming a sort of ethno-nationalist movement, often engaging in subtle or overt racism. This political vision is one where citizens are forced into compliance instead of choosing participation, usually brought about by an imagined Christian version of a strongman leader in the vein of Plato's philosopher-king.

To be fair, all governmental systems force compliance in some manner. But should the kingdom be forced on us? Or should it be something we choose? As Christians advocate for legislation, we must be thoughtful about these questions, for the measure we use to judge may be used on us. To put it plainly, there was a time when Baptists advocated for religious liberty because they were a persecuted minority. I remain grateful that those in power who were in the majority chose to show deference to my faith ancestors. Likewise, it is important for us to consider religious and demographic minorities in the midst of our own advocacy, because a measure of our faith is how we treat those with less power. As Proverbs 31:8–9 says: "Speak up for those who have no voice, for the justice of all who are dispossessed. Speak up, judge righteously, and defend the cause of the oppressed and needy."

Baptists have one theological contribution to history that serves us well in this discussion—the separation of church and state. From Roger Williams to E. Y. Mullins to today's SBC Ethics and Religious Liberty Commission, Baptists have long believed that coerced faith is not a true faith. This is why Christian nationalism (as an ethnonationalist movement) is misguided; it ultimately believes force can triumph over human hearts. Governments may be able to legislate actions, but they cannot legislate hearts. Such a governmental turn ultimately leads to an attempt to embody Christian law without the corresponding voluntary faith. That sort of move fails to account for how poorly people respond when they are forced to do something instead of choosing it freely. As the most recent version of the Baptist Faith and Message puts it,

"A free church in a free state is the Christian ideal."[8] Christians should advocate for their values in the public square. At the same time, it is wise to remember that we will be judged by the measure we use to judge, and we should advocate accordingly. We ought to embrace civic activity toward particular political ends, but we ought to remain suspicious enough of power in order to maintain a healthy prophetic distance. This is where—in my estimation—Christian nationalism fails most egregiously: it believes its imagined leaders to be impervious to the temptations of power.

To be sure, the United States (or any other global power) isn't going to embrace theocracy anytime soon. Likewise, the goal is not for Christians to seize power through political maneuvering, but it is instead for Christians to model how the kingdom of God subverts and redeems power by faithful witness to the kingdom. I believe the very best political action of the church is effective discipleship. As disciples multiply, communities are affected from the ground up. A multiplicity of disciples can care for neighbors and can support public policy to do the same.

The political vision I am proposing encompasses three big ideas: prophesy, embodiment, and participation. We prophesy truthfully so that we can point to the beauty of the kingdom, because the kingdom is Jesus's goal for the world. Only if we speak the truth of Jesus are we able to maintain our credibility. We embody an alternative vision of reality by living out the words of Jesus within the church. Those living within the way of the world will be best served if they can see what a different way of life might be as they gaze at the church. And we guide the state toward the kingdom by

8. Baptist Faith and Message 2000, section XVII, https://bfm.sbc.net /bfm2000/.

participating in the political processes afforded to us with an eye toward Jesus's redemptive plan for our world. Only as we do all three—prophesy, embody, and participate—can we connect to the cooperative, life-giving kingdom way.

＊

When citizens are given the power of governance by elected office or some other pathway, the temptation is to become consumed with self, to believe that those governing are more significant than those they are governing. At the same time, it is possible for those in the church to take the prophetic role to the point of hyper-criticism, of never seeing the benefit of government, of continually arguing that institutions must be reduced to rubble and completely rebuilt. When politics are at play, power quickly becomes the subject. If the governing or the governed are to find a way forward, they must find a common vision.

In Revelation 4, John describes the throne room of heaven. John sees the Lord seated on the throne and earthly rulers—elders—bowing before him. The elders have been crowned, presumably with earthly authority they earned during their lives. The elders, however, refuse to keep their crowns. Instead, they cast their crowns before Jesus. They do so willingly, recognizing that their greatest enjoyment into eternity is deflecting any self-glory and giving glory to the King of kings.

Our political lesson culminates before the throne: when we willingly deflect glory from ourselves and onto Jesus, we are crowning him King. This is the great call and challenge of the Christian church and its relationship to politics—we have a vision of the good life for human flourishing, but we cannot allow our desire to press that vision forward to be co-opted by the base desire to power grab. That would betray the very life we hope to create.

We must choose to instead believe and embody the following: the governed can be prophetic without becoming self-righteous. We do this through faithful Christian living and preaching. The governing can lead without becoming power hungry. We do this with an allegiance to Jesus over our own self-interests. Together we can remember that our goal is to recognize the kingdom as best we can, both within our churches and more broadly through civic activity. Together we can live an alternative vision of a cooperative and collaborative love for one another. This vision will not be complete until we find eternal glory in Christ, but we work diligently for it as we proclaim the kingdom today.

8

Black and White

Jesus on Race

This wound is in me, as complex and deep in my flesh as blood and nerves.

—Wendell Berry, *The Hidden Wound*

But a Samaritan on his journey came up to him, and when he saw the man, he had compassion.

—Luke 10:33

My oldest son and I got into my Ford Fusion to run some errands. It was a holiday Monday—Martin Luther King Day. The sun was shining, and the weather was pleasant. Houston summers are vindictively hot, but the rest of the year is usually quite nice. The radio was already on, and it was dialed to a news station. The commentators were doing a short piece on King's life.

I don't remember much about the piece itself. It was a standard historical overview, as I recall. But tucked away in that piece was a reference to overt racism and the damage it caused during King's era, continuing into our own. My son was listening quietly to the piece and then turned his head and asked me a pointed question.

"Dad, were you a racist when you were my age?"

I paused, thinking about how to answer this question. After just a moment, I answered.

"Sadly, I was."

"Did you ever use the n-word?"

I exhaled. My face began to turn red.

I reminded myself that healing begins with truth.

"Sadly, I did."

There is a day in the life of every parent when your child discovers that you are far more complex than they had ever believed, that you are not as good as they once imagined.

My son made that discovery on Martin Luther King Day.

The racism of my childhood was not the overt variety. It was not belligerent or mean. It did not speak ill of people because they were of a different ethnicity. It did not show its face in public—or if it did, it found ways to do so that were genteel.

The racism around which I came of age was the sort where people looked both ways before telling jokes. It was the sort where racial slurs were used in private company, never in the presence of people of color. It was the sort where race was never mentioned as a deciding factor in a controversial decision, even though most everyone involved knew that race was a deciding factor in said controversial decision. It was the sort of racism where interracial dating or marriage was frowned upon because people should "be with their own kind." It was the sort where we did not socialize with those outside our ethnicity. It was the sort where we did not worship with those outside our ethnicity. It was the sort where we looked down on the way other ethnicities looked, dressed, or behaved. It was the sort where we worked to preserve Confederate history without highlighting the history of the enslaved. It was the sort that used poorly reasoned statistics to justify itself.

It was, in short, a polite racism. It clothed itself not in brash epithets but with tradition, culture, and a pseudo-intellectualism. It told itself that it was acting in the best interests of everyone involved.

It was subtle, and it was insidious. It worked its way into me without my conscious awareness. This racism was so ingrained in me, so learned, that I am still discovering places where it holds ground within me.

I am ashamed to report that I was in college before someone told me that the n-word was not to be used, even behind closed doors.

I am ashamed to report that I once believed the Confederacy was something of which I ought to be proud. Heritage, not hate, after all.

I am ashamed to report that I did not learn about the Tulsa Race Massacre until I was in my forties.[1] I am ashamed to report that I did not learn about redlining until I was in my forties.[2]

1. In 1921, the Greenwood district of Tulsa, Oklahoma, was one of the wealthiest Black communities in the nation, popularly dubbed "Black Wall Street." In the wake of news that a young Black man would be lynched for assaulting a young woman, violence erupted, culminating in the widespread destruction of the Greenwood community, resulting in deaths, thousands of injuries, and approximately ten thousand Black residents becoming homeless. A 1996 bipartisan commission concluded that many city officials and White supremicists conspired with the mob to destroy the Greenwood district, resulting in millions of dollars of property damage.
2. Redlining refers to the banking practice of drawing red lines on a map to outline communities where loans and mortgages are commonly refused

I am ashamed, not because of my ignorance, but because I walked among Black friends and church members—fellow brothers and sisters in Christ—and did not think to ask about their lived experience. I was not curious enough about their lives to ask. I wrongly assumed their experience was the same as my own.

The racism I knew as a young man is the sort of racism described by Wendell Berry in his short masterpiece, *The Hidden Wound*. Berry insightfully notes that while our minority neighbors have borne the greater pain of racism, those of us who are white have been wounded as well:

If the white man has inflicted the wound of racism upon black men, the cost has been that he would receive the mirror image of that wound into himself. As the master, or as a member of the dominant race, he has felt little compassion to acknowledge it or speak of it; the more painful it has grown, the more deeply he has hidden it within himself. But the wound is there, and it is a profound disorder, as great a damage in his mind as it is in his society.[3]

Thank the Lord for grace.

Grace arrived in my life in the form of two people.

First: Blake Wilson. Blake is the pastor of a predominantly Black church, Crossover Bible Fellowship, about five minutes from the congregation where I serve. We met through a mutual friend, Skeet (which is the coolest name ever), one day over salads. Blake's church hosted a men's conference soon thereafter, and several of our men attended. From that moment forward, we became close.

---

because the area is poor. These practices have disproportionately targeted Black communities.

3. Wendell Berry, *The Hidden Wound* (Berkeley: Counterpoint, 2010), 4.

If memory serves, the men's conference was in February 2014. In August 2014, Michael Brown was killed by a police officer in Ferguson, Missouri. In the wake of the killing, a series of protests broke out in Ferguson and the surrounding areas. I can still remember seeing the images of stores, gas stations, and homes on fire. And I remember being very confused about the reaction. I spent several hours online trying to understand why this particular incident resulted in such a massive response. From my point of view, it seemed far too harsh.

Why would some people want to burn down their own town in response to a tragic death?

I didn't have any good answers, despite my research. Blake was the only person I felt comfortable asking that question. And, from there, he let me ask all sorts of questions. And he told me all sorts of things I had never considered. He told me about Tulsa and redlining. He helped me understand the stream of economics in the historical tradition of the Black church. He gave me perspective on why my Black neighbors—and other minority neighbors—might prefer attending a church that was almost exclusively made up of their demographic.

Second: Joel Goza. Joel is a white man who grew up in the church I pastor. When I met him, he lived in the Fifth Ward of Houston, a predominantly Black neighborhood near the center of the city. During his theological education, Joel discovered the problems of systemic poverty within urban settings. Along the way, he found that the historical Black church in America had a consistent prophetic voice on these topics, and he decided to devote his life's work to those streams of reconciliation and the eradication of poverty.

When I arrived at my church, Joel appreciated the work I was attempting to do, specifically as he heard my preaching on the kingdom. From time to time, he would reach out and encourage me. Joel pushed me to read more deeply in the Black theological tradition, particularly the sermons of Gardner C. Taylor and Martin Luther King Jr. He also pushed me to not settle for the status quo—or even for what I thought was "good enough."

As a white man, Joel had experienced my blind spots first-hand. He also knew the temptations to stop short of pursuing racial reconciliation, particularly for someone like myself who, in all honesty, could afford the luxury of taking a day off without thinking on this topic. But Joel saw the overlap of race and poverty every single day. That daily reality pushed him to an urgency that he pushed on me.

Blake and Joel, different as they are, both gave me a new set of eyes with which to see the issue of race.

Which gave me a brand-new way of reading the Bible.

The New Testament has quite a bit to say about ethnicity—broader than the dynamics of Black and white that dominate the conversation in the United States. I missed the scriptural message of multiethnicity as a young believer. The Bible is much like the world; we tend to see what we want to see. I wanted to see how God would save me, and so I did. But once I started looking for racial reconciliation, I found it almost everywhere.

The ancient Christian movement was, in the beginning, an almost exclusively Jewish movement. Jesus was Jewish. Jesus moved from village to village in Galilee, a region of Israel north of Jerusalem, teaching in the synagogues. His first disciples were Jewish fishermen from that region. When Jesus taught, the Jewish Scriptures were his text and his point of reference.

The Jewish people were, for the most part, an insular community in the first century. Yes, commerce from other regions, cultures, and peoples passed through Jerusalem, but, like most every people of that day, they stuck to their own kind. The Romans occupied the region, holding it in trust for Caesar, but Jews and Romans (and other gentiles, for that matter) rarely interacted. In one sense, they wanted to maintain ceremonial cleanliness; in another sense, it was simply the way people behaved. You associated with your own kind.

Reminds me a little of my hometown.

And yet Jesus pushed the boundaries of those who thought the kingdom ought to be limited to just one group of people.

In John 4, Jesus is traveling with his disciples from Jerusalem back to Galilee. The most direct route is through Samaria, but most Jews avoided that region. There was a long history of animosity between the Jews and Samaritans, dating back to the division of the nation into two kingdoms. The Northern Kingdom made Samaria its capital, and when it fell to the Babylonians, the people began to intermarry. The Jews of the Southern Kingdom (Judah) looked down on them as "half-breeds."

The Samaritans were rejected by those in the Jewish community of the day. I imagine there was more than ceremonial cleanliness on the line. As with most opposing groups, I suppose tensions would occasionally erupt into confrontations when the two groups came together. So it made sense for Jewish travelers to skirt the area on their way between Jerusalem and Galilee.

But that is not what Jesus chose on his journey. John 4:4 uses interesting language: "He had to travel through Samaria."

Jesus did not have to go through Samaria for the sake of expediency. None of his disciples would have thought it odd if he opted to take the long way around.

But, no, he had to go through Samaria.

I can't help thinking that's because he wanted to reflect the all-encompassing love of God toward all people—even the "half-breed" Samaritans.

In John 4, Jesus encounters a Samaritan woman at Jacob's Well. By the end of their conversation, he commissions her to tell everyone in her village about him. The entire village comes out to the well to meet Jesus and to verify her testimony that he might be the Messiah. Jesus does not run away or recoil in disgust. By all accounts, he sits with these people and stays with them, demonstrating the grace of God.

The kingdom is for every group of people.

If Jesus plays Texas Hold'em, he has a lousy poker face. He tips his hand again and again, showing us the trump card of a multiethnic eschaton at every turn. Jesus is not working for a monochromatic kingdom but for a jackpot featuring every nation, tribe, and tongue. Jesus knows that the grace of God is so surprisingly vast that he can't help but show his disciples: God wants everyone in on this game!

In each of the Synoptic Gospels, Jesus travels to the other side of the Sea of Galilee to a region known as the Decapolis, a collection of ten gentile villages. There Jesus performs perhaps the most well-known exorcism of all time. He confronts a demon known as Legion and sends the demon into a herd of pigs. After the demon has been sent away, the newly clean man wants to join Jesus, but Jesus releases him to go back to his hometown and tell everyone what God has done.

Jesus sits with Samaritans and commissions (former) demoniac gentiles.

And Jesus's confounding crossing of ethnic lines doesn't stop with these two encounters. He receives a Roman centurion, commending him for his faith when he wants his daughter healed. He heals the demon-possessed daughter of a Syrophoenician woman. Jesus crosses ethnic lines and religious lines, flouting concerns of cleanliness. He is not concerned with what others think of his promiscuous company-keeping. Rather, he gleefully gravitates toward those whom others would consider ethnic outcasts, showering them with public love.

His reputation as the friend of sinners (see Matt. 11:19) is well earned, but we might do well to think of him also as the friend of foreigners.

Time and again Jesus shows us: the kingdom is for every people.

Jesus's disciples received the message of the multiethnic kingdom loud and clear—even if they needed a little bit of reminding.

When Peter receives a vision in Acts 10, he is initially surprised. The Lord tells him to eat foods he has always considered unclean, and Peter initially refuses. But God has an important word for him: "What God has made clean, do not call impure" (v. 15). Peter soon realizes the vision is not simply about food; it is about people. When he is taken to the house of Cornelius, a gentile who is seeking God, Peter realizes the gospel is for everyone. And, perhaps in a surprise to everyone, the Spirit falls on each of them.

Meanwhile, Paul was carrying the gospel to so many gentiles that the first church council was convened to consider how to proceed with so many new gentile believers coming to faith.

In Acts 13 we get a snippet of information about the teachers and prophets in the church at Antioch, and we discover they are Jewish, African, Roman, and Greek.

The apostle John, in Revelation 7, receives a vision of the heavenly throne room and sees believers of every nation, every language, every tribe, and every tongue worshiping before the Lamb.

Peter, Paul, and John each follow the way of Jesus when it comes to the coming kingdom—it is for every single group of people.

And if that's the testimony of Jesus (and the earliest disciples), it seems that ought to be the testimony of today's churches. God's kingdom was multiethnic in Jesus's earliest visions, and God's kingdom will be multiethnic into eternity.

The sad reality is that the church in the United States continues to be divided along racial and ethnic lines in many cases. In an interview in 1960, Martin Luther King Jr. said, "I think it is one of the tragedies of our nation—one of the shameful tragedies—that 11 o'clock on Sunday morning is one of the most segregated hours—if not the most segregated hour—of Christian America."[4] Granted, there has been some movement on this front in American churches since 1960. There are certainly more multiethnic churches, and people of all ethnicities are welcomed (at least theoretically) into most congregations. At the same time, the fact that such a statement must be made with caveats tells us a great deal about the distance we have to go.

4. From an interview Martin Luther King Jr. did on the NBC television program "Meet the Press" on April 17, 1960. The clip, titled "The Most Segregated Hour in America," can be viewed on YouTube, posted April 29, 2014, https://www.youtube.com/watch?v=1q881g1L_d8.

Eternity will be multiethnic. The earliest churches were multiethnic in an age when xenophobia was high.

It seems clear: the multiethnic church is essential to the message of the kingdom.

Second Corinthians 5:19 says that God is reconciling all things in the world to himself through Christ. In the same passage, Paul says that those of us who are in Christ must be his ambassadors. As ambassadors, we have been given our message: reconciliation. We are to bring this message of reconciliation in Christ to the world, because God wants all the world to experience his glorious reconciliation. He is not interested in some neighborhoods being fully redeemed and others remaining run-down. He wants the all-encompassing riches of reconciliation to repair every nook and cranny of our nation and the world.

If we are ambassadors of reconciliation, if the church is to portend that which will one day be present, then we must be on the front edge of reconciliation in every area— but particularly on the front edge of reconciliation between ethnicities within the church. How can the church be an ambassador of a message if it is unwilling to live the message? I am writing these words just days after a man in Jacksonville, Florida, killed three people simply because they were Black. The shooter was a man in his twenties. We cannot believe the often-repeated trope that racism will die off as the younger generations come along. Young people are being racially radicalized every single day. The church must speak directly to these sorts of evils. To have any sort of credibility, the church has to look inward and bring reconciliation to bear on its own members. Physician, heal thyself first.

I once heard Mark DeYmaz, founder of Mosaic Church of Central Arkansas, put it like this: "God is not going to use the church to heal the race problem in America. God is going to use the race problem in America to heal the church." Mark is correct; before the church can speak prophetically regarding race, it must first look inward. The racial division within our nation is real, and if we are going to experience reconciliation, we need a church that has worked intentionally to bring about reconciliation within itself.

The gospel is the message of the church, and the gospel is the message of reconciliation. If the church is truly focused on this message of reconciliation, it can experience reconciliation inwardly and then, having healed, tend to the racial wounds of the world. I agree with civil rights legend John Perkins: "There is no institution on earth more equipped or more capable of bringing transformation to the cause of reconciliation than the church."[5]

Churches can experience reconciliation and, in turn, bring that reconciliation to the world.

———

Shortly after I moved to Houston, the Kinder Institute at Rice University announced that Houston was the most ethnically diverse city in the United States. This surprised me. I assumed New York City or Los Angeles would be the most diverse. But, no, it's Houston. Why is this? For one, Houston is close to the southern border. It is also a major port. Furthermore, Houston is one of the primary cities that receives refugees to the United States.

If I understand Houston's history correctly, the city began receiving refugees in earnest during the Vietnam War. One of the largest minority groups in the city are

5. John Perkins, *One Blood: Parting Words to the Church on Race and Love* (Chicago: Moody, 2018), 63.

those of Vietnamese descent. When the Taliban regained control of Afghanistan in 2021, hundreds of Afghans relocated to Houston. Situations like this result in migration to Houston on a regular basis. The world has found its way to Houston.

Sometimes Joy and I play a game when we go into the heart of Houston. We will listen to determine how many languages we hear in the course of an evening. One night we walked through the Galleria and didn't hear a word of English. As someone who grew up in a town with three primary ethnicities (and one Pakistani family), I still marvel at living and pastoring in a global city.

When I began to notice the citizens of the world coming to Houston, it took me back to the way I read the Bible. I began to think about the apostle John and his vision of the throne room. In Revelation 7:9 John says, "After this I looked, and there was a vast multitude from every nation, tribe, people, and language, which no one could number, standing before the throne and before the Lamb."

It was then that I realized something I never had before: John saw skin color in heaven.

I was raised in the era of "color blindness," when it was common for people to say that they didn't see color when speaking about matters of race and ethnicity. I understand the heart behind that sentiment, much of it likely born from pure intentions. But, if we're honest, the phrase was often used to sidestep thorny issues and to ignore cultural differences.

I love what John says. He saw every *nation*. He saw every *tribe*. He saw every *people*. He heard every *language*.

How can you see every nation, tribe, and people unless you notice their skin color, their hair, their eyes, and other features? You can't! John noticed that people from around the world were there in all their intentional, created glory. That is what God revealed to John in his vision.

And how did John know that there were people from every language unless they were speaking and singing in their native tongues? He didn't just *see* them. He also *heard* them. I love this. I imagine John listening to a chorus of global worship exploding into a fugue of dialects, with each tongue being distinct and yet somehow, miraculously, musically, cooperating in a supernatural harmony.

The people were each clothed in a white robe and waving a palm branch. The glory of humanity, created in the image of God, dazzled John.

Our God's love is so vast, so broad, so indescribable that it is for all people. Behold, Jesus is making all things new, including all people!

Sometimes when I'm in the middle of Houston, I'll think about John's vision. If heaven is where the nations find their completed redemption and sing in rapture, then Houston is a place that helps me picture that glorious choir—with every culture and melanin shade.

In Houston as it is in heaven, indeed.

As I read the Bible and saw the beauty of the multiethnic church, I was convicted. If the Scriptures envisioned a church and an eternity that were replete with the full spectrum of skin tones and the love of languages, shouldn't the church of this moment reflect that reality? And if so, what should our church do to help move that vision forward?

Our leadership began to discuss what it would look like for our church to reflect the demographics of the community. At the time, our congregation was right at 99 percent Anglo. Meanwhile, the nations had come to our city—and our community. I wanted to see our church change demographically, but I wasn't sure how to make that happen.

I'd like to tell you that we have had success story after success story on this front, but the truth is much harder and far more complex. Today our church is far more diverse. We haven't done any official demographic studies, but I would estimate we are around 30 to 35 percent non-Anglo on a Sunday morning. I wish I could tell you that change was simple and straightforward, but it has taken years of trial and error, years of mistakes, and years of learning for us to reach this point.

In all honesty, we are learning in real time how to be a church that reflects heaven—particularly in this area.

***

"What should I do to help diversify our church?" I was convinced I needed to do something and was pestering Blake Wilson for advice.

"Simple: preach the gospel," Blake replied.

I was skeptical. "That's it?"

Blake was completely serious. "If you preach the full gospel, people who are from a minority background will hear it and understand, and they will stay."

That was our first step toward diversifying our congregation—to preach the full gospel. In preaching the full gospel, we didn't stop at the salvation of the soul. We explained the kingdom—the way that believing the gospel affects every area of our lives. Racial reconciliation was part of that explanation.

Blake was right. Our church began to see more and more families from non-Anglo backgrounds attending.

I wasn't preaching on race explicitly, but I was certainly mentioning it from the pulpit on a regular basis, declaring that if our church truly believed in the gospel and the kingdom, then we should be a place for all people, no matter their ethnicity. The majority of my church agreed, but some apparently didn't, and they chose to leave.

I soon realized that my desire to create a multiethnic church was steeped in idealism, and my ideals would soon be shattered by reality. We're now about ten years along in our process of moving toward becoming a multiethnic church, and I've made far more mistakes than I ever dreamed possible. One of my pastor friends told me that dealing with race in the church is like climbing Mount Everest—possible but incredibly challenging. As we began our ascent from base camp, I realized just how accurate the analogy is. I made missteps regularly, seemingly sliding backward down the mountain's face.

Allow me to confess a few of my missteps. First, I underestimated how sensitive many people would be on this topic. To say that we want to address the issue of race can be heard as an implied attack—that we are racist, to be specific—and I unintentionally offended many right out of the gate.

Further, I didn't understand the difference between pursuing a multiethnic church and pursuing a multicultural church. Our church was ready to pursue multiethnicity, but the conversation surrounding a multicultural church, where a variety of cultural expressions are present in all levels of church, from organizational philosophy to worship expressions, is more complex.

Even further, as our staff became more diverse, I didn't account for how cultural backgrounds might result in misunderstandings, miscommunication, and accidental offenses. I didn't understand the cultural fluency I needed to navigate effectively among those diverse cultures.

And another: I failed to consider how cultural differences play into political preferences. Topics like immigration status and community policing are perceived differently by different cultural communities, and the best theological and pastoral responses to these topics are not always immediately clear—particularly for someone who has operated from a majority-culture mindset. On the Sunday after the George Zimmerman verdict was handed down, I remember thinking, "I no longer pastor an exclusively white church. I need to think about how to address this." Those sorts of thoughts never came to mind when our church was more homogeneous.

I could keep listing ways that I tripped up on this journey. The conversations surrounding race are so often intertwined with politics that even actions I took with the best of intentions were often misinterpreted.

Over the following decade, I received a lot of negative emails and comment cards and even a few death threats. Racism continues to be one of the most challenging topics I've ever attempted to address as a pastor.

And yet I would do it all over again.

The work is incredibly hard, but the payoff has been richer than any treasure.

When I see brothers and sisters in our congregation leaning into becoming brothers and sisters across ethnic and cultural lines, learning to love another in spite of perceived fears or difference, I begin to see glimpses of the forever kingdom. When I see my wife in the hallway pushing a Bye-Bye Buggy with six children from all sorts of backgrounds, I know the next generation of our church will be different. When we host events and worship translated into other languages, I know that we are looking more like heaven. When

I attend our church picnic and see our Spanish-speaking congregation excited to make authentic street tacos alongside the English-speaking congregation, which is excited to smoke brisket, I know we are making small steps toward reconciliation. When I receive an email from one of our Black families thanking me for acknowledging Juneteenth and recommending a Juneteenth documentary, I know we are helping brothers and sisters be seen.

———

Christians often refer to a verse that has become known as the Great Commission. Just before he ascended to the right hand of the Father, Jesus commanded his followers to "make disciples of all nations" (Matt. 28:19). For this reason, churches have been commissioning and sending believers all over the world for hundreds of years. We believe that God loves all people and wants to bring them into the kingdom.

In Houston, we don't have to board a plane to make disciples of the nations. God has brought them to us. This has changed our approach to church. We are constantly thinking about what it looks like to help our wildly diverse neighbors understand who Jesus is. And the more we do this, the more our church looks like our wildly diverse city.

Not every city looks like Houston. But I imagine most every city in the United States has some level of ethnic and cultural diversity. I also imagine that most of us want our churches to reflect the kingdom of God. To that end, I encourage each of us to take whatever steps we can toward reconciliation. As we reflect the ethnic diversity of the kingdom, we position the church to bring the healing message of reconciliation to the world.

I am not able to give a set of steps toward building a multi-ethnic church. Others have written such books. I would, however, point to the actions and words of Jesus and the apostles. I would point to the multiethnic vision of the New Testament, and I would challenge you to do whatever makes sense in your particular context. Perhaps it means a radical change in your church. Perhaps it means inviting someone over for dinner. Perhaps it means personal or corporate repentance. Perhaps it means reading, learning, and listening.

Whatever the case, let us not forsake the ministry that has been entrusted to us—the ministry of reconciliation.

At the end of the Bible, in the book of Revelation, John sees the tree of life in the heavenly city. The tree stands wide, its trunk crossing the river that runs through the center of the city. He describes it: "The tree of life was on each side of the river, bearing twelve kinds of fruit, producing its fruit every month. The leaves of the tree are for healing the nations" (Rev. 22:2).

I love this description.

The tree is singular, but it bears twelve types of fruit. The twelve types of fruit may be an allusion to the twelve tribes of Israel, or perhaps to the twelve apostles. But I prefer a different interpretation. Twelve is the number of completeness in ancient apocalyptic literature. Different types of fruit adorn the tree, representing diversity. Twelve types of fruit represents completeness in that diversity. In my mind, this tree is a picture of the kingdom—one organism made up of the completed diversity of God's creation. It is a picture of unity in diversity, and it stands at the center of the heavenly city because it is a living symbol of the kingdom.

And there on the tree are leaves with a very specific power. John tells us, "The leaves of the tree are for healing the nations" (Rev. 22:2).

In its unified diversity, the tree brings healing through what it produces. The fruit is delicious, but the leaves are medicinal.

I believe the tree of life points the way forward for the church. We are intended to be one in Christ, but we are not intended to be homogeneous. We are intended to be unified but not uniform. If we, like the tree of life, are able to live in a unified diversity, we produce something beautiful. Living this way reflects that which God loves, which Jesus loves. When the church does this, it embodies Jesus values in one of the most beautiful ways imaginable.

I believe that when we embody the kingdom, we will produce that which brings healing to the nations.

9

Royal Pain

Jesus on Suffering

He walked back into the woods and knelt beside his father. He was wrapped in a blanket as the man had promised and the boy didn't uncover him but he sat beside him and he was crying and he couldn't stop. He cried for a long time. I'll talk to you every day, he whispered. And I won't forget. No matter what.

—Cormac McCarthy, *The Road*

Or those . . . that the tower in Siloam fell on and killed—do you think they were more sinful than all the other people who live in Jerusalem?

—Luke 13:4

It was one of those phone calls that initially doesn't make sense. I heard the words Jon was saying, but I asked him to repeat them.
So he did.

He told me that one of the men in our church had been murdered by an escaped convict. Even worse, four of his grandsons were with him, and the convict had killed them as well.

I stood in my kitchen in stunned disbelief. This particular man was in his sixties. His family had been part of our church for over forty years. The boys had gone with him to the family property, just under two hours away, to help their grandfather and to do some fishing. During a botched prisoner transport, a convict escaped and eluded law enforcement for several days. As the convict looked for weapons and a vehicle, he came upon the family and brutally murdered them.

Joy and I were hosting some friends for dinner. We quickly excused ourselves and made our way to the homes of the family. At our first stop we saw the deceased man's father—who was in his nineties—and his brother. Their cries were guttural, almost primal. I don't remember much of what was said in those moments. What can be said in such a moment? We held one another and wept. I recall someone screaming out, "Why?!"

After some time we went to the home where three of the four boys resided. Their parents were crying and wailing. They lost their children in a single moment at the hand of evil. It was late by this point, but there were nearly a hundred people in their home. Tears or blank stares filled the faces of almost every single person. Deep, visceral pain filled the entire house and spilled out among the crowd gathered in the yard.

I remember those nights through a haze of grief. Certain moments are clear; others are cloudy. I said little beyond "I'm so sorry."

Hours later we circled with the family and prayed, sensing the peace of the Spirit but simultaneously feeling the loss of the boys.

In the coming days we organized the funeral, attempting to work with the press and comfort the family. Time passed from the deaths, but the suffering did not end. How could it?

The family had endured an almost unthinkable loss.

They were people of faith, but suffering visited them in the harshest of ways.

The question of suffering and evil has hounded those who believe in God for as long as people have chosen to believe. Religions have posited all sorts of answers to this particular question. Buddhism teaches that life itself is suffering made manifest and that part of our journeys must be to endure suffering and move past it. Nonreligious philosophies like hedonism have accepted the reality of suffering and argued that the best use of our lives is to pursue as much pleasure as possible.

The Christian faith has a unique struggle to overcome in the discussion of suffering, because it maintains that God is both all-powerful and wholly good.

Philosophers have long posed what is known as the question of theodicy: If God is good, how can there be suffering? Either he is not good, or he is not powerful. He cannot be both.

There is no neat and tidy answer to the question of suffering. To pretend as such would be pastoral malpractice of the highest order. At the same time, Jesus and the kingdom give us a way to think about and approach suffering that is not only unique but, in my estimation, the most realistic.

Suffering hits every single one of us; the way of Jesus provides the most complete way for us to move through it.

Suffering is difficult. It is painful. It is emotionally draining.

But, if the Jesus way is the right way, it might also point us to something glorious.

⸺

Suffering is inevitable. To be human means that you will experience pain. You will experience the death of a loved one; you will receive a frightening diagnosis; you will go through a painful heartbreak; you will grieve the loss of a season that was golden; you will hurt for your children; you will experience betrayal. Christians may not take the hard Buddhist line and flatly declare that life is suffering, but we would certainly say that suffering cannot be avoided.

Jesus himself said as much. In the hours leading up to his death, he told his disciples, "You will have suffering in this world" (John 16:33).

Pain will come, and it will often be creatively cruel. As a pastor, I have seen the wake of this cruelty more up close than I have wanted. I have seen leukemia take the life of a three-year-old. I have counseled a grieving woman whose sister and niece were murdered. I have walked down street after street ravaged by floodwaters, wondering how a city might be rebuilt. I have sat in the wake of stunning suicide. I have counseled teenagers grieving a friend who had a seizure, fell into a swimming pool, and drowned. I have held the hand of a woman as she took her final breath. I have watched the justice system release a known child molester.

Of course, not all suffering is acute. Some suffering is constant, wearing on our bodies and emotions, showing up in sleepless nights, chronic pain, a difficult child, a grinding job, or a taxing marriage. I've witnessed all of those as well.

I do not believe my witnessing these things makes me a hero. I mention them because witnessing these things shook me from my naivete. I used to walk blithely through life, oblivious to the pain of those around me. Pastoring shook me awake.

I am forty-eight years old as I write this. In some ways, my perspective on suffering is unique. But it is not unique in the world; it is not unique in my city. I realize I have seen more suffering than many of my church members, but I have not experienced nearly as much pain as many have.

The American church is in danger of ignoring suffering because it has that luxury. Our largest churches tend to be in wealthy suburbs, surrounded by nice homes and good schools. Our worship services in those churches tend to be upbeat, and the ministries tend to focus on families. The Christian radio station features a tagline: "Safe for the whole family." There is nothing wrong with any of those, but by focusing on creating a pleasant environment for personal growth, it is easy to ignore suffering. And let's be honest: even the comfortable theater chairs of the slickest megachurch are filled with people whose hearts are heavy with pain.

In those spaces, it is often easier to point to the positive than to sit in suffering.

We often ignore suffering because we have adopted a silent meritocracy. In the suburbs, there is an underlying assumption: if you work hard, you will be rewarded. The converse is also assumed: if you do not work hard, you will be punished. It's a very American way of thinking—our outcomes are directly tied to our effort. This is a classic free-market way of approaching the world, and our capitalistic minds can, if we are not careful, take the same approach with regard to pain.

I learned this firsthand when I was diagnosed with heart failure. There is something akin to shame in the eyes of people who encounter someone with a chronic illness. Perhaps they feel shame because they cannot heal you. Perhaps they feel shame because they know they will have a better life than you. But there is a small undercurrent of shame tied to wondering, "What did he do to deserve this? A pastor stricken by such a disease? God must be punishing him for something, right?"

Such thinking is akin to the prosperity gospel. The prosperity gospel teaches that we are rewarded financially for giving sacrificially to the church. Its tentacles spread to encompass all manner of spiritual implications. In a direct line from free-market economics to theology, you'll find people believing that if they do more for God, then they will reap greater blessings. And, just like the economic meritocracy of the suburbs, you'll find the converse: if people aren't being blessed—or if they're being punished—then they probably aren't carrying their appropriate spiritual weight.

This isn't a problem unique to the American suburbs. This way of thinking has been around for a very long time. So long, in fact, that Jesus ran into the same way of thinking.

In John 9, Jesus heals a man who has been blind since the day of his birth. His disciples are thinking along the lines of spiritual meritocracy—the man is being punished because of some unknown sin. "Rabbi," they ask, "who sinned, this man or his parents, that he was born blind?" (v. 2). Jesus is quick to dispel the notion that this is some sort of individualized spiritual punishment. His answer is to the point: "Neither this man nor his parents sinned" (v. 3).

On another occasion, people report to Jesus that some people from his home region of Galilee had been executed and their blood mixed with Roman sacrifices. Apparently, some thought that God was punishing those poor Galileans, but Jesus immediately dispels such a thought: "Do you think that these Galileans were more sinful than all the other Galileans because they suffered these things? No, I tell you; but unless you repent, you will all perish as well" (Luke 13:2–3). Jesus is explicit: They did not die because of some secret sinfulness. They died because Pilate was vindictive.

He then drives the point home: "Or those eighteen that the tower in Siloam fell on and killed—do you think they were more sinful than all the other people who live in Jerusalem? No, I tell you; but unless you repent, you will all perish as well" (Luke 13:4–5).

When tragedy strikes, Jesus says, it's truly a tragedy. God is not doling out public punishments for secret sins.

The same is true with blessings. In his Sermon on the Mount, Jesus reminds us that God allows good things to happen to people who certainly don't deserve them. He says, "For he causes his sun to rise on the evil and the good, and sends rain on the righteous and the unrighteous" (Matt. 5:45).

God has set up the world so that good gifts are given to all of us—things like sunrises, a baby's laugh, and the taste of a perfectly smoked brisket. Theologians call this common grace. God is gracious and good, and we all receive such gifts.

By the same token, we live in a world that is corrupted by sin. Choosing to follow Jesus does not give us special protection from the brokenness of the world. When we are born into this world, we are born into the mess, and the mess is hitting the proverbial fan. We're all going to get hit. That doesn't mean that we are being targeted for retribution. It means that every day we wake up in this world, we receive both a chance at beauty and a chance at pain.

This, of course, raises a question: If we receive both common grace and suffering whether or not we follow Jesus, then why follow him at all?

What benefit does Jesus bring to those of us who endure very real pain?

In February 2001, it seemed I might die. I had been diagnosed with heart failure about a year earlier, and my condition had deteriorated. The doctors decided my best bet was to be implanted with an experimental version of a pacemaker. Between the time the decision was made and the date of my surgery, I had to be taken to the hospital because my heart was in severe arrhythmia and failure. My condition was so precarious they kept me in the hospital until the surgery date.

One night, Joy and I were awakened by a scream from the room next to mine. It was the most hopeless wail I had ever heard. Nurses rushed into the room. We didn't peek into the room; we didn't need to. We knew the patient next door had died. I don't know who that woman was to the person who was now gone, but she grieved loud and she grieved hard. To this day I still think about that wailing woman.

I do not know that woman's story, but if I could describe her cries from that night, I would use the word "despair." She sounded hopeless, and she sounded all alone.

I have grieved much in my life. Most of that grief has been very public—deaths, for example. But there are a few things—losses I hold close—that I have grieved privately. Between the two, I prefer public grief. When you grieve publicly, you have the comfort of others. When you grieve privately, you experience all the emotions of grief, but since no one else knows your struggle, you are forced into an emotional wilderness. You have no comforter, no companion. This sort of grief is heavier; there is no one to help you bear your burden.

This is why Paul writes, "Carry one another's burdens; in this way you will fulfill the law of Christ" (Gal. 6:2). Paul knows this life is difficult. He knows that there will be times when we will need someone to help us carry this burden. I also think he knows there will be times when we will not have an earthly companion. That is why he says that carrying the burdens of others fulfills the law of Christ.

Jesus helps us carry the things we cannot carry. He is our companion when we have no other companions. He is the one who tells us that he will never leave us or forsake us (Heb. 13:5). I am reminded of the two disciples on the road to Emmaus (Luke 24:13–35). They felt completely alone and abandoned, and that is where Jesus met them and supped with them. There at the table, as the bread was broken, they finally recognized him in the breaking. If you, like me, have cried into your pillow, feeling completely alone, then you might need to be reminded: God is with you. He joins you on the road, walks with you, and sits with you at your table. And, like those two heartbroken disciples on the road to Emmaus, he meets us in the breaking. And it is there that we finally recognize him.

The grief of the Christian is very real. The pain Christians experience in this life is very real. We cry tears like everyone else. But in our darkest hour, in our deepest loneliness, in the loneliness that carries heartache and heartbreak, we are not alone. Jesus joins us there. This is the gift that the God made flesh in Christ gives—he knows heartbreak as well as we do. He was abandoned by everyone who loved him. He was tempted in the darkest of ways. He was killed by those who needed him most. And because he was heartbroken, because he was a man of sorrows (Isa. 53:1–6), he is a God who can be trusted with our deepest hurts and griefs.

This is the difference for Christians who grieve. We believe that in our deepest shadows the light of Christ shines on us.

When we feel most lonely, we are not alone. He is with us.

This is one of the most powerful truths of the Christian faith. Every person on this planet will experience suffering, pain, grief, and sorrow. The Christian holds fast to this truth: no matter what befalls us, we will never be alone. God is with us, and his presence makes a difference. Furthermore, we hold fast to the day of resurrection, to the day when Jesus will finally make all things new. On that day, we will know that our suffering was not in vain, that we were never alone, no matter how dark the valley of the shadow of death may have seemed.

My father-in-law was a pastor for fifty years. I've learned a great deal about how to pastor well by watching him. I don't think I know anyone in this world who does one-on-one pastoral care better than him. One of the first things he taught me about pastoring was how to make a hospital visit. His first rule? Be sure to sit down. He explained, "You may have a lot to do. You may be very busy. But when you sit down, you communicate to the person in the bed that you are willing to stop for a moment and enter into their world." I like that image—stopping and sitting. It reminds me of Jesus and the woman who anointed his feet with pure nard, or the Samaritan woman at the well, or the parable of the Good Samaritan. In each instance Jesus took time to be with the person.

This is the beauty of public grief: If we are willing to be vulnerable, to express our hurt, then those around us will come and bear our burdens with us, to show us Jesus. And when we bear the burdens of those who are grieving, we show the law of Christ.

We live in an age of achievement and hurry. When I imagine Jesus, I do not picture him in a hurry. I see him taking time to appreciate flowers and sunrises. I think of him stopping to talk with the people he met on the road.

Jesus enters into our lives, sits down, and joins us.

Another pastor friend once told me that when I encounter someone in a tragedy, I should—in spite of any temptation—resist giving any advice or spiritual platitudes. "You say two things," he said. "'I'm so sorry' and 'I'm praying for you.' Then you sit down and stop talking."

This is counterintuitive advice, particularly for those of us who make our living using words. We feel the pressure to say something profound, but our well-intended words often wound where we intend to heal. Rather than platitudes, then, we offer presence.

Have you ever had a friend who just sat with you in your dark moment? It's comforting. There's no need for words. Presence is enough.

This is what Jesus gives us when we are in the shadows of despair. He sits beside us. He puts his arm around us. He allows us space to weep, to scream, to question. But he does not offer empty answers. He does not give us a pep talk. He sits with us. And in the breaking, we discover him.

I've seen this presence manifest itself in my life and the lives of others in a variety of ways over the years. Most notably, I've seen firsthand the peace of God that surpasses understanding (Phil. 4:7) come over people—a calmness that people are able to maintain when their world is shattered. I've heard people describe this peace as simply being in shock or a shock response. I'm describing something different. I'm describing people who walk through a devastating event with a very real calm for days, weeks, or months with an assuredness of faith.

When one of the families in our church lost their three-year-old daughter to leukemia, Joy and I went to their home and sat with the grieving mother. She had theological questions, and she had very real grief. She also had a very real peace about her that I still sense, although her daughter has been gone for years.

We suffer, but God is with us.

And in his presence we are able to walk through suffering differently.

This is partly, I think, because the gospel reminds us that God identifies with our pain.

More broadly, however, I believe it is because the Christian knows God regularly redeems pain. The cross of Christ is the exemplar of redeemed pain. While Jesus cries out in excruciating pain, the cosmic forgiveness of humanity results. God walks through the deepest of pains, but suffering is not an end in itself. The cross serves as a reminder that God often does deep work in our hurt, sometimes doing a work that cannot be done without pain. God has worked in me at a deeper level more often during times of tempest than smooth sailing.

This redemption takes different forms. Most commonly, perhaps, we become empathetic to those who walk the road we once walked, and we strive to serve them. The grieving mother I mentioned earlier? She created a foundation that serves families who have a child with cancer. One of my favorite things they do: making portable birthday parties for kids celebrating a birthday while in the hospital. She did this because she watched her daughter spend her birthday in a hospital. She understood the plight of parents of terminally ill children because she had walked that road herself.[1]

Ideally, suffering tenderizes the tough heart, helping us better see those around us who are hurting. To be sure, suffering may embitter our hearts. I have experienced such a hardening in my life. Who could blame someone in deep pain for closing their heart to the world after experiencing betrayal, loss, or grief? But if we will allow God to do so, he can take our hurting heart into his hands and massage with the grace of his presence in the midst of suffering until it becomes soft again, until it opens to the hurt of the world. And when it becomes tender, our eyes are opened to the suffering of others.

This is the beautiful, countercultural witness of the church. When we live in the midst of suffering—walk *through* suffering—and allow it to make us kinder, more generous, more open to life, we are beginning to model that baffling way of Jesus. He knew that we would need to carry our respective crosses to know him, and in knowing him through suffering, he changes us. As he changes us, we live differently, displaying him in our pain. He is on display as the Shepherd bringing us through places we thought impossible to journey. And as we do so, the world sees the goodness of our Shepherd—our Good Shepherd.

We are each innately selfish, engrossed in our own worlds. I once heard esteemed music producer Rick Rubin say that

---

1. For more information, visit https://www.haleyshappybirthdays.org.

people are not accustomed to being truly heard.[2] I think the same is true when it comes to being seen. When we truly see someone else in the midst of their struggle, we rarely understand how much of a gift this is to the one in pain. It is a gift to see others who are hurting. And it is a gift to be seen. Life is so difficult, so painful, that we tend to build calluses to the pain around us as a defense mechanism. When we allow God to redeem our pain, one of the best things we bring is eyes to see the hurting around us.

What could be more like Jesus than seeing—truly seeing—those who are suffering? Jesus looked through gruff exteriors, ethnic and gender boundaries, and all manner of defense mechanisms in order to truly see people. That simple act of seeing brought redemption.

Ted Lasso reminded viewers, "Be curious, not judgmental."[3] Jesus was relentlessly curious about those he encountered. He sat, questioned, and refused to leave. He met people in their pain, and his act of seeing and meeting them changed them.

This is what God does. He walks with us. He understands us. He meets us. And he redeems that which we thought might destroy us.

Some suffering, however, feels irredeemable.

I opened this chapter with a heart-wrenching story of tragedy. That particular event is the most brutal thing I have experienced as a pastor, but I have witnessed the suffering of

2. I heard Rubin say this during an *On Being* podcast titled "Magic, Everyday Mystery, and Getting Creative," hosted by Krista Tippett, original airdate March 16, 2023, https://onbeing.org/programs/rick-rubin-magic-everyday-mystery-and-getting-creative.

3. Ted Lasso, "The Diamond Dogs," season 1, episode 8, directed by Declan Lowney, original airdate September 18, 2020, on Apple TV+.

many others. I've heard accounts of physical, emotional, and sexual abuse where the abuser walks away without justice being served. I've heard of the ravages of war and famine. Not all pain is able to be redeemed in our lifetime.

God meets us in our pain, and he comforts us, but we may not experience much beyond comfort.

At least not in this life.

And there lies another distinction of Christian suffering. When Jesus was raised from the dead on the third day, God proclaimed that death was no longer the final word on our existence. We will experience death—just as Jesus experienced death—but we will also be resurrected. The Christian gospel teaches that there will be a day when our dried bones will—like the bones of Ezekiel's valley—reattach, be joined with tendon and sinew, be covered with glorified flesh, and meet the Lord in the air (1 Thess. 4). According to the New Testament, this new life will never end and will be spent in the ecstasy of union with Christ as we revel in the new heavens and the new earth.

If the resurrection is not real, as Paul said, we are to be pitied (1 Cor. 15:14–20)—partly for deluding ourselves with fanciful notions and partly for thinking our pain will ever be redeemed. Those outside the faith might encourage us to grow up, to put on our existential big-boy pants, and deal with the inevitable conclusion: life is hard, then you die. Such views have been held for millennia. Narcissism, hedonism, and materialism spring from the fountain of such thinking.

But Christians have Easter Sunday hope, because Christians believe Easter Sunday actually took place. We believe in the resurrection.

On the day before I had my implantable cardioverter defibrillator implanted, I was reading my Bible, and God took me to Romans 8:11: "He who raised Christ from the dead will also bring your mortal bodies to life through his Spirit who lives in you." I suddenly knew that even if I were to die early, I would one day be alive again.

Encouragement washed over me. As did the peace of God that surpasses understanding.

If Jesus rose from the dead, then we will one day rise from the dead. If we will one day rise from the dead, then suffering will not have the final word over us. We will witness the death of death itself, and we will know that all of our pain has finally ceased. There will be no more weeping, and our joy will be made complete.

For this resurrection reason, Christians are able to endure suffering with at least two fresh perspectives.

First, we know that death does not have the final word. The reality of the resurrection changes hospital visitation. Over the years I have sat with numerous terminal patients who have, inexplicably, been joyful. I've watched them encourage the nurses and doctors. Shoot, they've encouraged me! While they know that their bodies will soon fail, they are convinced that one day their bodies will rise again. And because of that certainty of faith, they are able to stare down death without flinching. If I'm completely honest, I'm sometimes amazed at their faith. More than once I have left a hospital room thinking to myself, "I hope that when my time to die comes, I'm able to face it with that sort of faithful courage."

Belief in resurrection gives us a unique sort of courage. We believe God will defeat death, so while death may be painful, it will not be the end. Without a bit of hesitation, we can ask with Paul, "Where, death, is your victory? Where, death, is your sting?" (1 Cor. 15:55). Such courage reminds me of my personal hero in the faith, Dietrich Bonhoeffer. As the

Nazis led him to the gallows in the Flossenbürg concentration camp, he is reported to have said, "This is the end. For me the beginning of life."[4]

Second, if we believe in the resurrection, we necessarily believe in the final judgment. First Thessalonians 4 says that the dead in Christ will rise first, implying that all will rise from the dead. Revelation 20 speaks of the dead—great and small—standing for judgment, presumably after this universal resurrection. If that is in fact the case, then we can rest easy in the fact that every injustice that has been committed will one day be addressed. We may not see the man who murdered children or sexually abused women face justice in this life, but the resurrection assures us that there will be a day of reckoning. Without the knowledge of such justice, much of the world's suffering would necessarily lead us to despair. However, with the assurance of judgment, we can place our faith in a God who not only redeems our pain but also rights every wrong.

I have experienced things that seem irreparable. I'm certain you have too. The gospel means that there is not only good news of forgiveness and hope in this life and the next but also good news that justice will finally be administered, no matter what we have endured.

Perhaps the greatest surprise in Christian suffering is that, when done well, it actually inspires others—and sometimes even convinces them of the truth of the kingdom.

4. Bonhoeffer's biographer and best friend, Eberhard Bethge, reports that Bonhoeffer was leading a worship service as the guards came to lead him away. They burned the book manuscript on which he was working and led him to the gallows, where other prisoners reputedly heard him say these words. Eberhard Bethge, *Dietrich Bonhoeffer: A Biography*, ed. Victoria Barnett (Minneapolis: Fortress, 2000), 927.

My mother-in-law died from early-onset Alzheimer's. My father-in-law, my wife, and my brother-in-law worshiped the Lord at her funeral. They did so because they believe in the resurrection. And people were encouraged.

After twenty years of improvement in my heart condition, I recently experienced a relapse that may or may not result in the need for a heart transplant. Joy and I wept for several days, and then I was forced to consider whether I believe in the resurrection. When I decided that I do in fact believe in it, I was amazed how my attitude affected those closest to me.

That mother of the three-year-old who died from leukemia I mentioned earlier? Her insistence on redeeming her suffering for the good of those around her has resulted in more and more people believing in the beauty of the kingdom.

I do not believe that God brings pain into our life so that we might inspire others. I am not that deterministic in my theology. But I do believe that the gospel and the kingdom, when rightly believed and applied, can be used by God to redeem dark pain so that others might discover a fresh view.

Again, every single one of us will walk through the valley of the shadow of death. It is only a matter of time. The difference for the Christian is the knowledge that they do not walk through the valley alone.

The Good Shepherd walks with us through that valley. His rod and his staff comfort us. They do so because he never leaves us.

I am convinced that when we walk through the valley, we learn to listen to the Good Shepherd better than ever. I am convinced that it is then that we discover the true treasure of Christ. When I suffer, I am faced with a choice: Will I turn toward Jesus? Or will I turn away? I've done both over the years. I've chosen to turn away, growing harder and colder.

But I never saw that choice help me, and I never saw that choice help others.

Instead, when I've chosen—and seen others choose—to turn toward Jesus, I've seen redemption. I've seen them press into prayer and watched God open their hearts to the possibility of love. I've seen them allow their suffering to guide them to others who are hurting—through support groups, church ministries, and community programs. I've seen them use those connections to become Jesus to others who are hurting—to sit with them in their pain, to comfort them, and to remind them of the beauty of a God who never leaves.

If there is a beautiful thing in suffering, it is that it forces us to come to terms with loss. When we lose a loved one, a dream, a healthy body, or a life we once envisioned, we must grieve it. And then, in the darkness of our grief, we are better able to see the glimmer of our treasure. The gems of hope, resurrection, love, and the presence of Jesus come forward. Suffering well allows us to see that the only thing truly worthy is knowing a God who never leaves, who loves, and who stands with us in the midst of the darkness. The more tightly we cling to him, the more clearly we see that he is our treasure, that we are rich—even when all has been stripped away.

When the church surrounds those who are suffering, our great temptation is to offer platitudes: "Everything happens for a reason." "She's in a better place." "The Lord works in mysterious ways." But when we check our platitudes at the door and truly enter into the suffering of others, we find the beauty and power of the cross.

Most of modern Western life is about avoiding pain. When the church willingly comes around those who are suffering—

when Christians choose to enter into suffering—we embody the way of Jesus.

Earlier I mentioned Bonhoeffer's concept of vicarious representative action (*Stellvertretung*). When Bonhoeffer looked at the incarnation, the crucifixion, and the resurrection, he saw Jesus acting for a humanity who was incapable of acting for itself. Jesus freely chose to act in love on behalf of humanity because he believed suffering on behalf of another to be the only path of salvation—simultaneously demonstrating the very character of God to be self-giving love. Later, Bonhoeffer willingly endured a death sentence for his role in a plot to attempt to overthrow Hitler because he believed he was enacting *Stellvertretung*—doing that which others could not do on their behalf. He knew he might face temporal or eternal judgment for doing do, but he considered enduring such punishment similar to what Jesus did for humanity.

When the church chooses to suffer with those who are hurting, to help those who cannot help themselves, to enter into suffering in order to demonstrate the love of God, we display *Stellvertretung* and thereby enact the values of the kingdom.

I cannot conclude a chapter on pain and suffering with a tidy ending. I know that many of you are hurting at a level that feels indescribable. I do not come with a solution, but I come with the news of a God who will enter into your darkness. This is the God whose love is so vast, so profound, that he willingly enters into pain simply to demonstrate his desire to be unified with you.

Suffering often feels pointless. This world often feels cruel.

The resurrection, however, points us down a path where suffering does not have the final word.

The kingdom offers life here in a way that other avenues cannot.

If I could offer any pastoral advice to those reading these words who are in the midst of dark days, it would be to draw on that great truth. You may not have someone to support you in the flesh, but the Spirit of the living God is with you. Jesus is with you, holding out his scarred hands, feet, and side. He shows them to you to remind you that he knows the reality of pain. He shows them so that you know he has redeemed pain before, and he can do so again. He shows you his wounds so that you might know that those wounds did not have the final say over his body, and your wounds will not have the final say over yours.

He has never left you.

And he never will.

10

Get Busy Dying

Jesus on Finding Life in Death

Jesus said to her, "I am the resurrection and the life. The one who believes in me, even if he dies, will live."

—John 11:25

Then Jesus said to his disciples, "If anyone wants to follow after me, let him deny himself, take up his cross, and follow me."

—Matthew 16:24

One of my favorite films is *The Shawshank Redemption*. It tells the story of Andy Dufresne—a man wrongfully convicted of murdering his wife—and the men he meets during his time in Shawshank Prison. One of those men, Red, becomes Andy's closest friend. Just before Andy makes a daring escape from the prison, he has a conversation with Red that foreshadows his impending plan. Andy tells

Red that should he ever manage to get out of the prison he would head to a small Mexican town on the Pacific coast—Zihuatanejo. Although Red cannot envision a life outside of the prison walls, Andy has thought of nothing else. He has been working toward this end the entire time he has been locked up.

During this discussion with Red that focuses on the theme of hope, Andy delivers the film's most powerful line: "I guess it comes down to a simple choice, really. Get busy living, or get busy dying."[1]

We must decide how we will live, and then we must set about doing it, for we will all die one day.

Those of us choosing the kingdom life, however, may want to adjust Andy's charge to Red.

If we have seen anything in our examination of the kingdom, it is that the kingdom is counterintuitive. It does not surprise us, then, that Jesus would tell us that the best way to find life is to die to self. When Jesus told his disciples to take up their crosses in order to follow him, he employed the metaphor of death. Just as Jesus had to literally carry his cross to Calvary, enabling his own public execution, he tells his disciples that choosing to follow him means they must metaphorically carry the means of killing their own selfishness each day.

We must die to self, because we will desire things that are the antithesis of the kingdom. We will want to fear others, but the kingdom calls us to love our enemies. We will want to hoard our money, but the kingdom calls for generosity. We will want to divide into homogeneous ethnic ghettos, but the kingdom calls for multiethnic community. The list goes on.

1. *The Shawshank Redemption*, directed by Frank Darabont, written by Stephen King and Frank Darabont, Columbia Pictures, released 1994.

The kingdom requires death to desires that come naturally, that often seem like they would be for our best. But if Jesus is to be believed, then we often want things that would in fact harm our emotions and our souls.

Dying to self means that we stop seeing our lives, our theology, or our churches as separate from the world. The kingdom requires that we see ourselves as connected, as part of something much larger. When we die to ourselves, we assume a posture of cooperation, ready to share that which we have so that those around us might taste the life we have found at the Table. Dying to self allows us to no longer operate from a mindset of scarcity but instead to become people ready to give our lives to making a world in which Jesus is King and his way is honored so that all people can flourish.

In dying to self, we find the secret to living. At first I thought Jesus would rephrase Andy's charge to Red along the following lines:

Get busy dying so you can get busy living.

But after reflecting on the kingdom, I think it would be something more like this:

Get busy dying so you can get busy helping others live.

This is the final great paradox of the kingdom—it promises greater life, but it requires a radical death, a death to ourselves.

As the West becomes more wealthy and more selfish, I believe this self-denial will become more resonant and more urgent. When I can access any corner of the universe from a portable screen and have whatever product my heart desires delivered to my home within twenty-four hours (forty-eight if Amazon is having issues), I will inevitably experience the sort of emotional ennui popularized by French philosophical theorists.

If I can have everything, I will eventually feel nothing. If I feel nothing, I will work to feel something.

Some will turn to substances or sex. Others will turn to militarism or activism. But in this moment of emotional emptiness, the call of self-denial will open a door of return into the kingdom. I believe that many will find the joy of self-denial to be the path into the kingdom that will reinvigorate the call of Jesus. There, in the death to self, future generations will find life. There they will discover again the beauty of the kingdom.

This is where love resides—in the self-giving love where I view the world through the lens of connection and cooperation rather than as a zero-sum competition. The reductionistic thinking of competition will eventually kill us, because our mistrust and separation will move us to the brink of self-annihilation. The only path with a chance of success is the path of the kingdom, because it is a path where we choose to love God and neighbor in a way that will force us into creative solutions. There we can bring out the old treasures from the Scriptures and the new treasures of creative solutions. There we can look into the past and see into a different future.

The kingdom is the place where obedience is not drudgery but joy. The kingdom is the place where choosing to love brings us into the place where we find, sustain, and multiply life.

The kingdom is our only path forward, because the path of competition has been worn into a path too hard for seed.

We need fertile ground, a place where a small seed of love might grow into a flourishing life.

Jesus's way is the only possible way forward if we want a hopeful future.

In Matthew 13:52, Jesus says that those who discover the kingdom are like people who have old treasures and new treasures in their storehouses. They have the old treasures because they know the things God has always valued. They have new treasures because they see the way to live as they repair the world through the kingdom.

When we seek the kingdom first, we will find treasures old and new. We will be wealthy and satisfied, for we will have found the things of true value, the things that give life.

STEVE BEZNER (PhD, Baylor University) is senior pastor of Houston Northwest Church in Houston, Texas. He is a local leader and participant in Multi-Faith Neighbors Network, where he builds bridges with Muslim and Jewish communities. Steve also serves as a board member of the Houston Church Planting Network, trains church planters through Glocalnet, and is an adjunct professor at George W. Truett Theological Seminary. He is married to Joy and has two sons.

 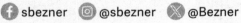